Just One More Day in the Driver's Seat

5-12-12

My Dearest Vicky

Life is a Precious Gift from the Lord Above - Cherish the Memories and our Loved Ones Tomorrow is Not Guaranteed - Every New Dawn is another chance for hope - to Believe in a Cure. Keep the faith. Love & Blessings

Nanci

i

Just One More Day in the Driver's Seat

my son's journey
through DSRCT

Nanci Rainey

TATE PUBLISHING
AND ENTERPRISES, LLC

Published by Tate Publishing & Enterprises, LLC
127 E. Trade Center Terrace | Mustang, Oklahoma 73064 USA
1.888.361.9473 | www.tatepublishing.com

Tate Publishing is committed to excellence in the publishing industry. The company reflects the philosophy established by the founders, based on Psalm 68:11,
"The Lord gave the word and great was the company of those who published it."

Book design copyright © 2011 by Tate Publishing, LLC. All rights reserved.
Cover design by Erin DeMoss
Interior design by Christina Hicks

Published in the United States of America

ISBN: 978-1-61346-821-0
1. Religion / Christian Life / Death, Grief, Bereavement
2. Self-Help / Death, Grief, Bereavement
11.12.01

Near us is a celestial spirit, who, from the cradle to the tomb, does not leave us for an instant, guides us, protects us as a friend, a brother; will always be a consolation to us especially in our saddest moments.

—Padre Pio

This book is dedicated in loving memory of
William Thomas Rainey III.

when Billy came home totally exhausted from what was to be a relaxing camping trip, telling us horror stories of his nightmarish experience. He and Jeremy were in their tents when the forest ranger approached them in the early morning hours and rather sternly insisted they move their campsite to another location. Evidently, the site they had chosen was considered a restricted area, and by the time they packed up and relocated their camp, they were left with little time to sleep. All in all, Billy was grateful for the time spent with his friend, as Jeremy was leaving for boot camp the following week.

Billy graciously accepted an invitation from Jeremy's family to accompany them on a road trip to the Great Lakes for Jeremy's graduation from boot camp at the end of the summer. It was a long drive, and when Billy called me to let me know they arrived safely, I could tell he was extremely tired. He said the trip had been difficult; he was a little cramped in the car, and was experiencing pain in his abdomen. He remembered feeling some discomfort the day before he left, thinking he may have pulled a muscle while lifting a heavy piece of equipment. I told him he could take an aspirin and get a good night's sleep, hoping he would feel better in the morning. The next day he said the pain persisted, and he found a lump in the groin area; he thought it might be a hernia. He said he was able to tolerate the discomfort until he got home. Two days later he returned home, and we scheduled an appointment with the doctor, who diagnosed it as a pulled muscle, and he prescribed an anti-inflammatory drug. He said Billy could return to work with no restrictions, but if he didn't feel any better within a couple of weeks, he should return to the doctor. The following weekend, shortly after Billy retired for the evening, he was vomiting, had diarrhea, the shakes, and chills. He was weak and in extreme pain and actually asked to go to the hospital. The emergency-room physicians took X-rays and gave a diagnosis of bilateral hernias and recommended we see a surgeon. Since Billy's dad previously had two hernia repairs, we contacted his surgeon for a consult.

Billy's appointment with the surgeon was scheduled for October 10, 1997, at eight o'clock in the morning. I accompanied him to the office but did not proceed into the examining room due to the sensitive nature of his symptoms. I sat in the waiting area for Billy to return. Billy finally entered the reception area with a frustrated look on his face. Leaning toward me, he said, "Mom, this guy doesn't think I have a hernia. He said there might be something to do with lymph nodes or something."

Well, that's all I needed to hear. As soon as someone mentions lymph nodes, it's like waving little red flags. Upon hearing Billy's words, I immediately became panic stricken. I froze in my seat. I took a deep breath, composed myself, and responded, "Come on. Take me to work. I'll see if I can get you an appointment with Dr. Mike. I'll call him from the office." Dr. Mike was a well respected, general practitioner in a nearby town, referred to me by my mother.

"Mom, I'm not going to any more doctors. This is getting ridiculous. First it's a pulled muscle, then two hernias, now it's not a hernia, but they don't know what it is. It's probably nothing. I'll be fine. It's just gotta take time. I pulled something at work, that's all."

Disregarding my son's dismissals, as soon as Billy dropped me off at the office, I made a phone call to Dr. Mike's office and left a message requesting an appointment for my son. Within the hour, I received a call back from Dr. Mike, stating he had an opening and would be willing to see my son if I could get him there within the next hour. Immediately I called Billy at work and gave him the directions to Dr. Mike's office. A bit agitated that he had to see yet another doctor, Billy complained that he had already missed an hour's time of work that morning, and if the other doctors didn't seem overly concerned, why should he be?

doctor suggested we take Billy to one of the more prominent hospitals in Philadelphia for further diagnoses. He recommended Jefferson for renal care and/or the University of Pennsylvania Hospital for urology treatment. He trusted we would have more-conclusive information after they obtained the biopsy.

Prior to undergoing the biopsy, Billy was examined by a gastroenterologist, who reported no Gl disorders present. The surgeon who performed the biopsy said he was able to make a small incision to remove a nodule for testing; he also removed four cups of fluid. When Billy was returned to his room that afternoon, he was in a lot of pain and concerned as to what the biopsy would reveal. He was given pain medication and something for anxiety, which made him groggy. Billy was asleep when the doctor returned with preliminary biopsy results and said Billy was suffering from a type of lymphoma. Devastated by this news, I was glued to Billy's bedside and knew I couldn't leave the hospital. Billy's father went home to be with our other children, while I spent the night in a chair I pulled up beside Billy's bed. I was there when he opened his eyes and asked for more pain medication. I stayed by his side and told him I would make sure the nurses would get him whatever he needed. I promised to remain there as long as I was allowed.

The following day, Billy needed two units of blood and continued to ask for pain medication. Although the official biopsy results were not yet back from pathology, the doctor now felt we were dealing with some sort of a sarcoma, which, he explained, was a growth of tissue between the organs. He offered to make some telephone calls and consult with oncology specialists in the Philadelphia area and get back to us with more information. In the meantime, he discharged Billy and said he would call us the following day with referrals.

On Friday, October 17, 1997, we received a telephone call from Dr. Mike after he had discussed his findings from the preliminary biopsy report with a hematologist at Jefferson Hospital.

Both concluded we needed a soft-tissue specialist. He said it was within the realm of possibility that Billy would be referred to an oncology specialist most likely in the city, or wherever we could get the best treatment for him. At nine o'clock that very evening, we received a telephone call from Dr. Michaels, an oncologist at Thomas Jefferson University Hospital. She explained that our family doctor (Dr. Mike) had briefed her of Billy's status, and she did not feel we were dealing with a sarcoma. She said the cells described were not components of a sarcoma, therefore, she thought it might be a carcenoid, which may not be highly malignant and is often accompanied by low-grade abdominal pain. She suggested we bring Billy in for an examination, along with the pathology slides from the biopsy. We agreed to see Dr. Michaels on Monday, October 20, 1997, at eleven o'clock.

When we arrived at Dr. Michaels's office, she performed a thorough examination, asking Billy several questions relating to change in appetite, fatigue, pain in his lower back, fullness in his abdomen, change in bowel or bladder habits, etc. She agreed to review the pathology slides and said she would consult with a group of specialists to determine Billy's diagnosis. Offering us a brief moment of optimism, she advised that not all tumors were highly malignant and that they could be treated in stages. Our goal was to find the origin of the tumor and any other possible areas where it could metastasize. Since Billy's blood pressure, temperature, blood, and urine cultures were all fine, she did not feel further laboratory work was necessary. After reviewing the CT scan and X-ray films, she felt the tumor was surrounding the ureter to the right kidney and there was a tumor behind the intestines and around the bladder. She believed the tumor originated in the front of the rectum and moved forward. She suggested Billy had a fairly large tumor. There was no kidney damage yet, but she felt we must move quickly. Her first inclination was to shrink the tumor via chemotherapy. She would, however, consult with the pathologist and radiologist at Jefferson before determining the next course of action. Panic stricken, we went home, awaiting the doctor's phone call with further instructions.

Billy and I talked on the way home. "Mom, do you understand what they are saying?"

"No, Billy. They aren't even sure of what they are dealing with. First they have to determine what kind of cell it is. Then they have to find out what organs are involved and how large it is. Then they have to determine how to treat it."

"Mom, do I have cancer?"

"Well, that's what they are trying to figure out. Some cancers are treatable with chemo or radiation, and then you're fine. With other cancers, they have to operate and remove the tumor, and that's all. We just have to find out what it is. Sometimes it's a tumor or something non-cancerous. It might not be malignant."

"What do you mean?"

"That means it is just a tumor or a lump or something benign. They can treat it—it isn't cancer."

"Oh." Billy was quiet for a moment.

"Let's just hope it's something like that. Let's just pray that it's something simple that can be taken care of quickly. You'll be fine, Billy. You eat healthy, you exercise. You're in good shape. You'll be fine. Don't worry. I love you."

My mind was racing. *Tumors, chemotherapy, what is happening here? Billy is sick, but my son does not have cancer, does he? How could he? Billy is only eighteen years old. What is going on? Is this a bad dream? Oh, please, dear Lord, this can't be true. I beg you. Hear my prayers. Please heal my son. How can they tell me my son has cancer? Why don't they know for sure? This is a mistake, right? Dr. Michaels will call me back later with better news. They were premature in their findings. The test results must be wrong.*

We were all frightened with the mere mention of cancer, and my heart sank at the thought of chemotherapy treatment. I couldn't grasp such a diagnosis, and Billy's younger brothers, Matthew and Sean, were confused; they didn't quite understand the disease or the treatment process. Up until that time, cancer was something that happened to other people, never dreaming that would be something our family would have to face. I tried my best to explain to the boys that nothing was certain at that time. I was struggling. I knew I was losing control of the situation, and it was imperative that, as a family, we pray for healing. Silently, I prayed to the Holy Spirit for the courage to hide my uneasiness and for the wisdom to allay their fears. Somewhere deep inside the chambers of my heart I knew we needed a miracle. My faith had carried me through so many rough patches in the past. The Lord had always provided. We had always managed to find a way to make ends meet, always finding the means to feed our family. My faith had sustained us in the past, and I was convinced my faith would once again spare us and my son would be cured; everything would work out fine. I knew Billy would be all right. He had always been so healthy. I tried to stay calm and comfort Billy. I told him not to panic and that we couldn't jump to conclusions; we just had to wait for that phone call. In the meantime, we prayed—prayed to our dear Lord that He would watch over Billy and protect him. We prayed together as a family storming the heavens that everything would be just fine.

The phone rang at eight o'clock in the evening. It was Dr. Michaels. The X-ray results showed the tumor was unreceptive, whatever that meant. She believed Billy's diagnosis was a very rare cancer called desmoplastic small round cell tumor, DSRCT in short. The origin of this disease is usually unknown. It is very rare; there were only fifty cases published in *The New England Journal of Medicine.* She had some knowledge of DSRCT through a pathologist in New York who had first described this disease and wrote a protocol for it. She went on to explain that DSRCT has three components to each cancer cell: ectodermal (carcinoma), which develops in the tissue and skin; muscle type (sarcoma); and neural (carcinoid), which damages nerve tissue. She was not sure which component was the stronghold in Billy's case—that had to be determined. She said her main concern was Billy's right kidney. It was not totally obstructed, but if they didn't shrink the tumor, it could have posed impending damage. There was no determined cause for this disease, though she said it was not hereditary. This disease required extreme doses of chemotherapy and high amounts of radiation. The downside was the kidneys and bladder couldn't tolerate the high amounts of radiation needed to effectively shrink the tumor. She advised treatment begin immediately. Her nurse made the necessary arrangements for Billy's hospitalization, and we were told to report to the hospital the very next day. Stunned and in shock, I hung up the phone. I let out a loud cry, and Billy and the rest of the family gathered around me and anticipated the outcome of the phone call from my reaction. With Billy by my side, I clung to him and cried and said, "Oh, Billy, Billy, I am so sorry. It is cancer. You have cancer. Billy. My Billy. This has to be a mistake. They can fix this. They have medicine. You'll see. They'll fix this."

We all cried, holding onto each other for comfort. I called my mother and told her the results of Billy's tests; she immediately drove to my house. Within fifteen minutes she was there praying with us. We began to pray, "Please, dear Lord, heal our son. Make Billy better. Bless our family. Bless Billy. Heal us, please, please O Lord. Hear our prayer. Amen." Our prayers continued to calm us, and our tears eventually stopped. We each took a deep breath and knew our love and our faith would heal Billy. Yes, our faith would heal.

I didn't sleep at all that night. I don't know how Billy slept. I couldn't imagine him getting any sleep at all. How could he? He was terrified. How could I help him? How can a mother tell her son he will be all right when he was just told he had cancer? How can a mother say, "It's all right. We'll make it better," when this is something out of her control? The sting of reality had just slapped me in the face. I was completely powerless for the first time in my life. We were dealing with the monster of all monsters. We were faced with the biggest obstacle of our lives, that repulsive, dreaded word *cancer*.

Billy's hospital admittance was arranged for eight o'clock in the morning on October 21, 1997. We arrived at Thomas Jefferson University Hospital and went directly to the third-floor admissions office. After submitting our insurance information and signing release forms, we were escorted to Billy's room. Many medical students and interns visited us during the first few hours subsequent to Billy's admission. An urologist examined Billy and ordered a renal scan and Lasix washout. He described the procedure for the renal scan, explaining dye would be injected intravenously to view the kidney function; the Lasix washout allowed them to watch the kidneys fill up and follow through with the draining. After the tests, Billy's creatinine level was 1.0, which was normal. Billy had good blood flow, but the right kidney was not draining well. The doctor suggested a stent be placed in the ureters to allow the kidneys to drain properly into the bladder.

An oncology fellow, Dr. Cristo, known as Rocco, also went in to examine Billy with Dr. Michaels. He further explained the multidisciplinary, P-6 protocol written by Dr. Brian Kushner at Memorial Sloan-Kettering Hospital in New York, regarding DSRCT.[1] They suggested surgically removing as much of the tumor as possible, which might have included removing parts of the intestines, and, worst-case scenario, Billy would have needed a colostomy. If the tumor invaded the ureters, the doctor indicated a urostomy would also be a possibility. The doctor saw a puzzled look on Billy's face and explained that the urostomy would basically be an external pouch connected to the bladder for urine collection. Billy and I exchanged glances, at which time I held his hand as I looked at the doctor for reassurance that this would be a last resort. The next step would be chemotherapy.

The protocol suggested Billy would begin chemotherapy two weeks after surgery, which would consist of seven high-dose, inpatient treatments every three weeks. If necessary, radiation may also be considered. We were warned of the side effects of the chemotherapy, including hair loss, nausea, vomiting, infertility, and the possibility of the chemo causing yet a different cancer in later years. We were also advised that a surgical procedure to insert a double lumen infusaport in Billy's chest would also be necessary for the administering of the chemotherapy drugs. This would prevent Billy from getting stuck in the arm or hand several times for his chemotherapy treatments and would also allow the nurses to administer his medications intravenously through the same port. We were overwhelmed with all this information. We were at the mercy of the doctors at this point, as we knew we had to act fast. We had to get Billy on the road to recovery and soon. I'm not sure who was more scared and confused, Billy or me. Regardless, I spent the night in his hospital room, sleeping on the window seat, taking notes of everything they were saying. It was all foreign language to me at this point, but I was determined to learn everything I could about my son's care.

At 6:35 on Wednesday morning, October 22, 1997, the nurses went in to prep Billy for his stent placement. They explained to Billy that the stents were used to open the ureters. The anesthesiologist required release forms to be signed and explained the anesthesia process to both Billy and me. The urologist also went in prior to surgery, explaining that after reviewing the tests and CT scans, he felt there was a good possibility he would have to insert bilateral stents. He advised that the procedure would not take too long and said I could wait for Billy in the holding area. He said we needed to eliminate any further kidney and bladder problems before we attempted the chemotherapy. At seven fifteen, they took Billy down to the operating room. I was able to go down with him until they administered the anesthesia. I kissed Billy good-bye and good luck and waited in the family surgical waiting area. At nine o'clock, Dr. Shur told me the surgery was successful. He did have to insert bilateral stents, Billy was in recovery and doing just fine. At ten o'clock, Billy and I returned to his room. He was in pain and nauseous.

At eleven o'clock, a surgical intern examined Billy and reviewed his medical history. He explained that the surgeons had consulted with the oncologist, radiologist, and pathologist to determine the best course of action. Dr. Michaels had been in contact with Dr. Kushner from New York and had consulted with Drs. Rosa and Berber, the surgeons recommended to us. Dr. Berber visited Billy after reviewing the films and told him it appeared to her that the tumor was eating the entire colon. She said she'd try to piece it without having to perform a colostomy. On a good note, she did say the inside of the bladder looked fine. She also indicated chemotherapy was Billy's only life-saving method at that time, and in her opinion, we had no other choice. We had to shrink the tumor before it did any further damage to the organs. Once they were able to shrink the tumor, she would surgically debulk it from Billy's abdomen.

Dr. Michaels went to see Billy in the afternoon. After hours of consultation with the team of experts, it was the consensus tumor debulking be done as soon as possible. The team did not feel we had time to wait for the tumor to shrink via chemotherapy without causing more organ damage. Surgery was scheduled for the next day. Dr. Berber returned to Billy's room at five o'clock that evening and explained the surgical procedure to him in detail. Billy's team of doctors relayed their concerns that if the areas affected by the tumor were not removed, a hole would form during chemotherapy. The operation, called a laparotomy, was an abdominal incision through the midline, in which the surgeons would remove the tumors and any affected organs. In her words, Dr. Berber explained there was a lot to treat and one of the more serious risks of this type of operation was blood loss. Therefore, an infusaport, which was more of a permanent IV line, would be inserted into Billy's arm, enabling the staff to administer blood products, medicine, and nutrition. She informed Billy that he would most likely receive his daily nutritional supplement, aka TPN, through the infusaport. This TPN would contain vitamins, minerals, and lipids calculated specific to Billy's body chemistry. Prior to the operation, they had to get Billy's colon as clean as possible through several Fleets enemas. The cleaner the colon, the less likely he would need a colostomy. The doctor said it appeared the tumor was resting on the back of the rectum very close to the colon.

Billy was then asked to sign the consent form. He looked at me, with his big brown eyes, questioning whether he should sign. I nodded, and he signed the form. Later I told him that the doctors would most likely be giving him forms to sign for every procedure since he had reached the age of consent. "Mom, what if I don't sign the consent forms? Will they still operate?" Billy asked.

"Well, Bill, I don't know. There's a good chance they'll persuade you to sign, or they might even ask me to sign. More likely they'll tell you if you don't sign, you'll be putting your life in danger, blah, blah, blah."

"So I should just sign? Maybe I'll try to refuse one of these times," he said with a smirk. Then he said, "You know, Mom, I'm going to get a tattoo."

I asked him, "Where did that come from?"

And he answered, "Yeah, on my butt, and it's gonna say, 'Exit Only.'"

I just looked at him, puzzled, and then I figured out what he was referencing. He had a grin on his face, and I started to snicker. Then we both laughed. At least he was able to find some humor in what he was dealing with. I know how much he hated those enemas. We were laughing, but deep down inside, my heart was breaking, and I know he didn't mean to be witty. He was as terrified as I was.

The urologist later returned to Billy's room and told us a catheter would be required after surgery, and since the stents were foreign matter in the body, the risk of infection was greater.

Therefore, he would be on heavy-duty antibiotics. For the next few hours, several residents and interns from various departments examined Billy. He was so frustrated having to review the events of the past few days over and over again. "Don't these people read the charts?" he would ask. I reminded Billy that it was a teaching hospital and it was up to the students to question the patients and not look into their charts. By the time the fourth student went in and asked for his history, Billy's body language indicated he was getting ready to explode, so I promptly gave them Billy's background, reading everything I had scribbled from my notes.

It was time for Billy's meds, so I asked one of the nurses to give Billy his Ativan, which helped him sleep for about an hour, because at ten o'clock a CT scan of the lungs was ordered, and Billy was off again on a gurney down to radiology. Fortunately, all the lung fields were clear. It was an exhausting day for Billy. His body was shaking, and he was scared. We all were. Although I was by my son's side and able to hold him, I continued to feel so completely helpless. All I could do was tell him how much I loved him and assure him that our prayers would be answered. Thursday, October 23, 1997, ten days after the initial CT scan, Dr. Michaels arrived in Billy's room with an article published by a pathologist and colleague of Dr. Kushner, regarding the type of tumor we were dealing with and the P-6 protocol.[2] She also gave me a copy of a letter sent to her regarding Billy's care from Dr. Kushner requesting she keep him informed of Billy's progress. Dr. Michaels also allayed some of our fears when we were told that Dr. Berber had done hundreds of bowel resections and similar types of surgery comparable to Billy's. Although Billy's tumor was quite rare, Dr. Berber had never performed surgery removing this specific type of tumor. She also informed us of the psychiatric services available to assist us in coping with this dreaded disease but said we must first and foremost, debulk the tumor. The anesthesiologist went into the room and explained the general anesthesia he would be administering in addition to epidural anesthesia. Billy was given pain medication and Ativan to help relax him until surgery. Although Billy was on the surgical schedule for noon, the operating room was not quite ready for him. It wasn't until one o'clock in the afternoon that transportation arrived for Billy.

Tumor Debulking

T he clatter of the stainless steel castor wheels wobbling across the linoleum floor resonated through the corridor. Billy and I exchanged glances. I reached for his hand, knowing they were coming for him. There was a loud tap on our door. "Patient transport." Our nurse entered the room; she was accompanied by a gentleman in his mid-forties, wearing green scrubs. They verified Billy's patient-identification bracelet then assisted my son onto the stretcher, placing a blue three-ring binder at the foot of the bed. The nurse wished us well while the escort gave the rear wheel a quick kick with his foot and backed out of the room. He turned the bed through the doorway and headed down the hall toward the patient elevator. Taking quick strides to keep up, I walked next to my son, resting my hand on his shoulder. When we exited the elevator at the seventh floor, we followed the nurse into a small holding area with curtain partitions. Another nurse acknowledged our arrival with a nod and pointed nonchalantly to the second cubicle. The escort applied the brakes on the bed then signed the paperwork fastened to a clipboard as he muttered, "Have a good day."

I dragged a small, metal-framed chair with a light-blue leather seat across the floor, resting it next to the bed. Before I sat down, I leaned over Billy and brushed my fingers through his hair. I reminded him of the prayer chain initiated by family and friends and we had to place the hands of our surgeon in God's care. He nodded, and together we recited the Our Father, Hail Mary, and Glory Be and then our novena to Padre Pio. I looked deep into his beautiful, brown eyes and promised I would stay with him as long as the doctors permitted. I also assured him I would be there the moment he awoke. I continued holding his trembling hand as I lowered myself into the chair. I took a deep breath and closed my eyes for a second before resuming our conversation. I tried to direct the dialogue toward his strengths and talents, but we were interrupted by the commotion beyond the pale yellow curtain. We could hear the beeping of IV pumps and the automatic door buzzer. From under the curtain, we viewed a parade of stretcher wheels accompanied by white clogs, sneakers, and an assortment of shoes. One particularly odd pair of scuffed clogs caught my eye. I pointed them out to my son, and we guessed the gender of the wearer, giggling afterward when I poked my head through the curtain for the answer. We continued with our diversion until the doctor entered the room to administer the anesthesia. The surgeon greeted us with a compassionate smile, shook my hand, and gave my son a high-five. The OR had been prepped, and they were ready to begin. I kissed my son on the forehead, told him I loved him, and followed him as far as I could. The nurse slid her ID card through the security panel on the door, and upon crossing the threshold with the stretcher, the doors abruptly closed.

As Billy was escorted to operating room two for a laparotomy and tumor debulking, one of the nurses took me to the family waiting area on the eighth floor. Billy's dad, Nicole, and my mother were already waiting there. When I joined them, we prayed and waited for what seemed to be forever before we heard any news from the doctors. Hours had gone by, and the nurses could only tell us the doctors were still working on Billy and had no news to report yet. They suggested we get something to eat or drink in the cafeteria. Hesitantly, we did go to the cafeteria, bringing our food back to the family waiting area in fear of missing the doctor's call. Shortly after the dinner hour, Billy's support team had grown; his friend Kevin arrived, along with my sister, JoAnne; my sisters-in-law, and Billy's boss's wife, Maureen. We were told the operation could take five or six hours, but we had approached the seventh hour, and still no word. At seven o'clock the waiting area had to close for the evening, and we were asked to go to another waiting lounge on the seventh floor. It was a much smaller room, but we were able to find seats at opposite ends of the hall. This gave me the opportunity to pace, and for another hour we all paced and prayed. Finally, at five after eight in the evening, one of the surgical nurses came out and reported that they were able to remove all the tumor. All the tumor, all of it! I had never been so happy. "Oh, thank You, Jesus," I cried.

We were told Dr. Berber would be out to speak with us after they closed Billy up. At 8:40, Dr. Berber sat with us and told us they removed a fifteen-pound tumor. She had never seen anything like it. The tumor filled the entire surgical basin. They had to remove the entire sigmoid colon, entire large intestine, and most of the bowel because they were deteriorated by the tumor. Unfortunately, they also performed an ileostomy, which is an external bag attached to his abdomen to collect body waste. We were told there was a chance the ileostomy could possibly be reversed at a later time, perhaps after chemotherapy and radiation treatment. Although Billy and I were both advised there was a possibility an ileostomy would be necessary, it was Billy's biggest fear that he would really have to deal with a bag attached to his stomach. Once the doctor gave me the news of the ileostomy, I barely heard anything else she had to report. My only thoughts at that time were how I was going to explain this to Billy. I knew he would be devastated by this outcome. I do, however, remember her saying they left about three tablespoons of tumor on the spleen, which was also enveloped with tumor, but hoped they would spare the spleen and the chemo would kill the diseased cells. There was tumor left on the entire lining of the diaphragm, but the diaphragm is such a thin surface they couldn't scrape any further without possible damage to it. The entire surface of the bladder was filled with tumor, and they had to perform major bladder resectioning, which included dissecting almost every nerve in the abdomen. As a result, Billy might experience some bladder dysfunction. She did see some bladder contractions in the OR and felt that was encouraging. In her opinion, after the chemotherapy treatments during a second-look operation, they may be able to reverse the ileostomy, possibly connecting the ileum to the rectum, forming a "colon." She did not insert the infusaport at that time. She felt it better for Billy to recuperate from the procedure and then operate again a week to ten days afterward for the port placement, if Billy's vital signs were good. He tolerated the operation well, yet all I could do was cry. Everyone said he was going to be fine, but I only envisioned my son's body dissected and invaded with cancer cells. All I heard was "hoping chemotherapy would destroy cells that were left." I was overwhelmed at what they had done to my son. I never imagined them finding such an invasion in his abdomen. It was too much to absorb. I knew I had to meet with the doctor later and write it all down. It was much too much for me to hear at that moment. I needed to get to my son. I had promised him I would be there. I just had to get to him.

The nurse let me in to see Billy at ten o'clock. I held his hand, kissed his forehead, and told him I loved him and that he would be fine. He opened his eyes and gazed into mine with fear and pain. The first words he uttered were, "They took my colon, Mom. They took my colon." There was total silence. My lips couldn't form the words to tell him he would be okay, that he made it through the surgery. I just looked deep into his eyes and wiped away his tears. To break the silence, the rest of Billy's support team was permitted in the room to see him for just a moment. The staff was so kind to let them all in. Billy then went to the intensive care unit, and I had to wait in the family area until morning, pacing the floor and praying.

Over and over again I pleaded, "Oh, please, dear Lord, make my baby fine. Save him. Spare him from any further disease. Let this be the end. Kill the rest of the cells. Oh, I can't believe this. All his organs? This can't be true. How can he have cancer? How did this happen? This can't be. Please, oh, dear God, all the angels and saints, dear Mother of God, my Mother, Mary, please intervene. You are a mother; please help my son. Padre Pio, I'm calling you. Please, I beg you."

Postop

Despite all the medications and heavy sedation, Billy was still unable to get a full night's sleep. He had IVs in both arms—three lines in one arm and two in the other. The GI drains were attached, and Billy was getting a bolus (which is the maximum dose of medication prescribed at one time) of morphine every two hours. He was having severe stomach pains and was very nauseous. Even though the NG tube was in (a tube that was passed through his nose and down through his esophagus into the stomach that was supposed to remove the stomach fluids from surgery), Billy continued to spew bile through his mouth and cough up mucous. The nurse put the GI drain back on continuous and immediately called the doctor. An oncology fellow went down to see Billy, and he was greatly concerned by his severe discomfort. He told us that he would talk to the oncology team and suggest they bump up the morphine on a continuous basis through the PCA pump, which we both found to be a pain in itself because in order to get what they call a hit of medication, you had to push the button. This pump was set to disperse a specified amount of medication at specific intervals, but the patient had to physically depress the button in order to release the medication. This became a real problem for Billy because when and if he would finally fall asleep, he was unable to push the button to dispense the pain medication. It just didn't make sense to us. Rather than Billy having control over the medication, it seemed the medication pump had control over Billy in that he had to remain awake or even alert enough to "demand" the bolus. I wasn't playing games with the machine and made sure I hit the button when it was time. The nurse explained that the pump was designed so the patient could be independent with his pain meds, which would probably work as long as the patient stayed awake. I felt sorry for patients without family by their side. The medical fellow said there was no reason why Billy should have to suffer so much and assured us that he would review Billy's medication chart and make necessary recommendations to the team. He seemed sincere and apologized for the ongoing discomfort and urged Billy to contact him personally at any time if there were any further problems or concerns with his pain management. Eventually the doctors changed some of his medications, and Billy was able to get more sleep. Within a few days, he began to show signs of improvement.

Remarkably, by the third day, even though the doctors didn't think it was time to remove the NG tube, they did agree to move Billy from the ICU to a regular room on the surgical floor. Everyone was glad to see Billy out of the intensive care unit, and he was never without company. His boss, Bob, came with his son, Bobby, both a little apprehensive to see Billy so far removed from his element; they couldn't even imagine seeing Billy lying still and certainly not seeing him in a bed with tubes. This was the first time Bob was able to get to the hospital, and Billy was anxious to see him. They had a great time talking about the yard and how things didn't seem the same without Billy. That was

"Mom, remember when the doctors came in for their rounds? Remember what they said? They told me the more I moved, the stronger I would get and the sooner I could go home. I just wanna go home, Mom. I just wanna get out of here and go home."

I remembered exactly what happened that afternoon when the doctors made their rounds. They were amazed to see Billy up and about and quite pleased with his motivation and energy. They did tell him the more he moved about, the stronger he would get, and one of the very first questions Billy asked was "When can I drive?" Billy was itching to go home and regain his independence. He was feeling confined in the hospital and trapped by all the apparatus, especially the ileostomy pouch. He just wanted out. The doctors encouraged Billy to continue walking, but he had to be patient. He was making such great strides in his recovery, but he was still a ways to go before being discharged. One of their greatest concerns was to get Billy to tolerate solid food. This was just his first day on liquids.

During the next week, I continued to spend the nights at the hospital on my usual window seat bed. Once Billy began to show some steady progress, I would go to the office for a few hours. The firm was so compassionate and flexible with me. There were days I never even went to the office, and on good days, I would spend a few hours there. I would return to the hospital at lunchtime and spend time with Billy, and if he was feeling okay, I would go back to work for another three hours or so and then return again to the hospital for the night. Many dear friends and relatives would alternate visiting with Billy on the days I did work. Nicole and Maureen would alternate days, and Kevin would spend a few evenings with Billy. On the nights Kevin would stay, I would go home and touch base with everyone and get them up to speed with Billy's progress. Matthew and Sean would either be at my mother's house or with friends. It was extremely hard on the boys, having me spend so much time at the hospital, and it was even harder for them to see their brother so sick and in the hospital. On the weekends or days off from school, they would join me at the hospital and spend the nights there as well. Each of us learned to sleep on whatever chairs were around. If necessary, we would find an empty chair in the hall and roll it into Billy's room. The nurses would bring us sheets, and if we were lucky, sometimes we would even get pillows.

As soon as Billy was able to sit up in bed, he asked Kevin to bring a camera to the hospital. Once it was determined he was suffering from something so rare and he would be following an experimental protocol, he wanted to document every step of his progress. He began to take an interest in the research we found online and was curious as to the progress of the other published studies. He was determined to beat this thing, and he wanted each phase documented with photographs. We were all surprised at this request because Billy wasn't much for the camera, however, Kevin and his mom went right back to the hospital that evening with a camera, and the snapshots began.

As a result of so many doctors and medical students observing Billy's surgery and following up on his recovery, Billy seemed to be more comfortable with his scars. I suppose that was his way of confronting the beast; he looked it straight in the eye and dealt with it. He was going to beat this, and he wanted to document every drain, PICC line, and scar that he endured.

Six-hour Pass

B y this point Billy was quite anxious to go home. He was able to shuffle up and down the hall, but with obvious fatigue, and it had been so long since he had a decent meal. Although the dietician cleared Billy to eat just about anything he wanted, he still wasn't able to tolerate food; nausea still had the upper hand. The doctors encouraged a high-calorie diet and ordered milkshakes throughout the day, but he couldn't tolerate those either. Finally, a CT scan was ordered and was negative for any possible blockage, so the doctor reinstated a clear-liquid diet for Billy until the nausea subsided. This dietary setback brought on another bout of depression and frustration.

During these low moments, Billy urged me to stay by his side. His frail body was invaded enough, and he did not want the doctors and nurses to probe him any further. If there was something that needed to be done, he requested that I be the one to do it; of course, I indulged him. It was my mission to make my son comfortable. He had endured so much, and if I could lessen even the slightest amount of pain, I would do whatever it took. I promised him we would conquer this together. I pleaded with Dr. Berber to do anything in her power to expedite Billy's discharge. A few days later, Billy was steadily eating solid food, yet the team became concerned with his depression. I told them he needed to get home if even for a day. He just needed a break. They decided to honor Billy's request to leave the hospital, but only for a few hours. After many days of persuasion and the kindness of very dear doctors, arrangements were made for a six-hour pass home the following Saturday, provided Billy's blood counts were at acceptable levels. The last thing we needed at that point was any type of infection.

You can't even imagine how glad Billy was when he found out he was going home, albeit six hours, but he was going home. We quickly made plans for Billy's homecoming with friends and family. My mother prepared a traditional Italian holiday dinner from soup to nuts. Billy was in his glory. He was so grateful just to sit and watch the Eagles game in the comfort of his own home, with his brothers, cousins, and, of course, Kevin. Although he wasn't able to eat much, his appetite was satiated with the delectable aroma of Nan's home-cooked food. I remember having tears in my eyes while watching Billy interact with his family and friends; he seemed to be truly at peace for the first time in months. We knew the freedom was only temporary. However, it was the best decision we had made.

It is noteworthy for all those in the medical profession to consider some of life's simple pleasures in lieu of conventional medicine when and if it's at all possible. There is much to be said about taking a leap of faith and trusting one's instincts. Billy wanted more than anything in the world to be home, and thanks to one courageous, deeply compassionate doctor, quite an unconventional prescription was written for Billy, a six-hour pass, one small act of kindness and a great leap of faith. I truly believe Dr. Berber was listening to the whispers of an angel that day, and I will be eternally grateful. We all knew there were risks involved

Homeward Bound

Day fifteen postop from the tumor debulking, Billy was discharged from the hospital. You can probably imagine how happy he was, not to mention how excited and relieved his brothers and sister were. This was a glorious day for all of us. It was a wish come true. We arrived home by two o'clock in the afternoon. Kevin wanted to be there the minute Billy got home and was so excited to see him when he emerged from the car, which made Billy's homecoming fantastic. He was so grateful to finally be in his own home, surrounded by family and friends, all of who were hoping for a routine lifestyle for Billy.

The hospital staff had made all the arrangements for home delivery of any medical equipment and TPN supplies we might need. The home infusion nurse arrived later that afternoon and reviewed what seemed to be hundreds of forms and every aspect of home health care. Billy was assigned a regular home-care nurse, Ryan, who had formerly worked at the hospital with chemotherapy patients but had transferred to the Jefferson Home Care division. The initial plan was for Ryan to come twice a week—on Mondays so that he could change the PICC line and again on Thursdays to take Billy's lab work (blood counts, etc.). Upon the aide's initial visit, we were again inundated with forms and file folders containing information about the home-care nursing program and several contact phone numbers in case of emergency. .

Billy had more visitors by the time the nursing visit ended. He was particularly happy when Uncle Joe stopped by with Nan. Uncle Joe always seemed to brighten his day. Billy was always intrigued by his big-truck adventures and was anxious to join his uncle for an outing. Once Nicole came home after work, we were finally all together. We hadn't been together, the entire family, since our six-hour pass. The day we had waited for was here. Although we knew there would be a whole new set of rules to follow for Billy's home care, everyone was ready and willing to help.

Our first night at home went smoothly. The TPN pump flowed without incident, and to my surprise (and Billy's), I even managed to flush the port line with heparin in the morning. By noon on day two, Billy had another visiting nurse stop by to take vital signs, and, of course, she had more forms for Billy to sign. The nurse asked about Billy's appetite and again stressed the importance of a nutritional diet. We had only been home twenty-four hours, but Billy was tolerating his meals. Friends and neighbors continued to visit Billy once they found out he was home.

Billy rested between visits, and after dinner, he expressed an interest in getting out. He and his dad decided to go for a ride to the local pizzeria. This was Billy's first piece of pizza in months, and he truly enjoyed it. He still did not have his appetite back, but whenever he felt he could tolerate a particular food, we tried our best to get it for him. He wasn't able to eat the entire slice, but he was able to digest what he did eat. Being outside was a taste of freedom for Billy. He began to feel more energetic, and his spirits were beginning to lift. It was just on this second day home that he asked his sister to take him to the barber the next day so he could get, in his words, "cleaned up." It was great to see him have some incentive to go out. The next day, Nicole did indeed take Billy to the barber, and to our surprise, he came home with his head shaved. It appeared as though he was no longer afraid to talk openly about his illness. He explained to the barber the nature of his illness and the ordeal of his operation. He said he was about to undergo a round of chemotherapy treatment, and he wanted to shave his head now before the chemo took its effects on his hair. When Billy's cousins Joshua and Jason heard of what he had done, they too went and had their heads shaved in solidarity. Billy grinned when he saw them, and they gave one another a handshake then a hug. I know he could feel the love. If memory serves me correct, I believe Kevin shaved his head as well. They all hung in there for Billy. He had a great support team.

The next few days, Billy continued to get visitors, and when he was feeling well enough, he would venture out. After getting approval from the doctors, when Billy was no longer taking pain medication, he was able to drive. He was thrilled to get behind the wheel of his Trans Am. He was cautious, though, and never went too far.

I can remember the first time he drove to the stone yard since his surgery. He came home so excited because, while he was at the yard, Rudy, a former welder, had stopped by. Rudy, who recently conquered a brain tumor, had by chance planned his day to go to the yard and ask about Billy, and as fate would have it, this was the very same day Billy decided to visit the yard. Both Billy and Rudy were pleasantly surprised to see each other. I truly believed that was divine intervention. Rudy was a positive role model for Billy, and the fact that he was able to overcome the brain tumor gave Billy hope. More importantly, Billy now had someone who could relate to his illness firsthand, someone he could talk to. I don't think Billy was comfortable talking about his illness to just anyone, and I know he had a lot of questions and a lot of fears.

Understanding DSRCT

As soon as we were given a copy of the P6 protocol, we immediately began our research on the specific medication and dosages, with particular interest on the side effects and contraindications.[3] There were dozens of pages of information detailing the specifics and sequence of the stages. The most devastating data we found was that the current mortality rate for DSRCT was five years. According to the initial studies, in order to have a fighting chance, it was vital that this protocol be followed precisely. One of the first articles given to me was a personal history found on the Internet, regarding a patient, Hayley Hendricks.[4] Hayley, a young girl from Nevada, was a student in the eighth grade when she was first diagnosed with DSRCT. Her initial symptoms were very similar to Billy's. She started with tenderness in her belly, first assumed to be a bowel obstruction. After the usual testing and radiological studies, it was determined that Hayley had some type of a metastatic cancer in her liver, and a biopsy showed that it was a rare cancer. After some quick research, the family found the Primary Children's

Medical Center in Salt Lake City, where there were five pediatric oncologists on staff, and they felt comfortable that this was the best facility for their daughter. Again, further tests were completed at PCMC, and another biopsy was taken on her liver.

It wasn't until four or five days later that Hayley was diagnosed with DSRCT. Their doctor immediately communicated with Dr. Kushner in New York, who had followed twelve patients with DSRCT.[5] They immediately started Hayley on a five-day course of chemotherapy drugs, ifosfamide and etoposide along with mesna. The family then returned to Las Vegas, and their oncologist worked with Dr. Kushner and set up a protocol, named P-6, which is high-dosage chemotherapy. This protocol had to be reviewed and approved by institutional review boards. Hayley's surgery followed her third course of chemotherapy.

Billy's treatment would differ slightly from Hayley's, only because his surgery was prior to any chemotherapy. His tumor was fifteen pounds and life threatening. The surgeon quickly determined after Billy's first admission to Jefferson that we did not have enough time for chemotherapy. Our research proved there were alterations in the P-6 Protocol, and the high-dose chemotherapy protocol was followed with slight variations. Dr. Michaels assured us she would be following Dr. Kushner's protocol and that she had been and would continue to communicate with Dr. Kushner throughout Billy's treatment. We were confident in our physicians and satisfied with their ability to follow Dr. Kushner's plan here in Philadelphia. It was also comforting to see other patients across the United States and Europe following Dr. Kushner's protocol and hoping for a better prognosis.

Along with the many med students and physicians involved in Billy's treatment, I too jumped at the chance to read every piece of research found on DSRCT. Because we were following the protocol of Dr. Kushner, I tried to keep abreast of the published progress of his case studies, absorbing as much information possible in the hopes of piecing together the DSRCT puzzle. What I didn't understand, I would ask the doctors; and when the protocol varied in the studies, I wanted to know why. Many doctors and students at Jefferson had a great interest in Billy's diagnosis and treatment. For some, this was the first they had heard of DSRCT. Being a case study, though, had as many disadvantages as it did advantages. In addition to all the attention and sometimes imposition on one's privacy, there was much trial and error and absolutely no guarantees. Needless to say, Billy was becoming a familiar face and his name well known in the Jefferson medical community. Because of the rare nature of this tumor and it being unfamiliar to so many physicians, Billy was frequently interviewed by medical students and doctors. He was most annoyed when he had to repeat his history and symptoms over and over again. There was limited research on DSRCT. As a matter of fact, the *New England Journal of Medicine* had only fifty documented cases. In addition to my quest for answers and the many tedious hours of searching through articles on all the different types of cancer cells, friends and family members joined me in my search. Most of the articles were full of medical jargon far advanced for our comprehension, saturated with chemistry terminology differentiating cell types and gene compositions. Skimming through these articles for a better understanding of the diagnosis and treatment procedures was quite a task. Much of this information was inconclusive, and it was evident that further research was still needed and this tumor had uniformly poor prognosis. One particular article found on the Internet, "Genetics of Small Round Cell Tumors of Children" by Mohammed Akhtar, MD, FCAP, FRCPA and M. Anwar Iqbal, PhD, FACMG, explains that the

> DSRCT tumor represented a heterogeneous group of neoplasms which are histologically characterized by undifferentiated small round cells which usually included malignant lymphoma, Ewing's sarcoma, rhabdomyosa-

rcoma, neuroblastoma, Wilm's tumor and desmoplastic small round cell tumor.[6]

The article further states,

> Desmoplastic Round Cell Tumor (DSRCT) is a rare tumor generally encountered in young adult male patients. The tumor usually presents as a hard multinodular mass, which is histologically characterized by a nesting arrangement of undifferentiated round cells associated with marked desmoplasia. Most of the tumors are located in the abdomen and pelvis.

The article continues with brief descriptions of malignant lymphoma, neuroblastoma, rhabdomyosarcoma, Ewing's sarcoma, and Wilm's tumor. Each of these different types of tumors played some sort of role in the diagnosis and prognosis of my son's illness. The terms and phrases included in these articles required a medical dictionary in one hand and the Internet close by for further definition and explanation. It was all too much to comprehend and interpret for the untrained, yet, faced with the reality of this disease attacking my son, it was impossible to just accept what the doctors were telling us; we had to know more. Within our search, we did find a few articles of personal histories of current patients stricken with DSRCT. We were particularly interested in their stories summarizing the diagnostic process and their treatment protocol. Most of these people had very similar histories of symptoms and diagnostic studies. For the most part, they too were following Dr. Kushner's protocol with some variations in the chemotherapy and radiation. Most of the medical articles revealed a very poor prognosis, with an average mortality rate of five years, but these few patients' stories were encouraging and gave us some hope. On January 28, 1998, we found two histories of particular interest to us. David Denault submitted an update to his history, and I quote,

> I was told by my oncologist that if I had a good response to my initial chemotherapy I might be expected to survive 20-24 months. I didn't have a good response to my first chemo; I'm still going 49 months after diagnosis. I'm not disease free, but I'm still going. [7]

Another, submitted by Andreas Dietrich and Maria Schlegel, writes, "What Dr. Honegger told (and keeps telling us), is very worrying, but not hopeless. 'I would' he said, 'not propose this treatment to you if I didn't believe there was a chance.'"

Of course, we did come across a few case studies and personal histories that were not very encouraging, but we put them in perspective and tried to focus on the positive results. We knew firsthand that this tumor was so complex and difficult to analyze and that no two cases were alike. Each person faced with DSRCT had experienced slightly different reactions to the treatments. Each individual treatment program was slightly altered, but for the most part, they followed Dr. Kushner's protocol. It was encouraging for us to read about these other patients' experiences, and some of them were optimistic and gave us hope. Billy was confident we were going to beat this thing. He was getting some of his strength back, and he was ready to fight.

There was a lot of information for both of us to retain. I had been keeping a notebook from the beginning of Billy's illness once we realized we were dealing with a rare tumor and forced to see so many specialists. This notebook became a vital tool for me. I was now documenting every doctor visit, vital sign, diagnostic testing, and surgical procedure. I was also taking note of Billy's pain scale and dietary issues. If there was any downtime, I would even recount some of our conversations, our concerns, and some of the emotions we were both experiencing. We were dealing with so many issues it was beginning to get impossible to remember everything the doctors discussed, and, believe me, there were so many doctors. Our list of healthcare professionals began to increase on a daily basis. By week two postop, we were dealing with social workers, dietitians, nutritionists, and various home health-care aides. We needed training on the IV pump, the TPN pump, and ostomy care. I was even informed I would have to learn how to give my son certain injections once we returned home. I was overwhelmed listening to the doctors and nurses explain signs and symptoms, medicine and ancillary items, words, and medical terms I had never even heard of. I had medical supplies and equipment orders to complete and I wasn't familiar with half the equipment they were referencing. I had no experience in the healthcare industry. I was a rookie at best.

It was a lot to learn, but Billy had faith in me, and I in him. Together we would do this. I continued to write everything in my notebook, which, at that time, was my survival guide. Some of the nurses laughed and joked about my extensive notes, but they also agreed that it was a good idea, as there were so many details to remember. I kept the book for my son's safety. It was too risky to make a mistake with his care.

Chemotherapy Preparations

During the evening hours, Billy and I would take walks through the hospital corridors. Sometimes we would even venture down to other floors. I tearfully remember one particular evening when Billy asked me why bad things happen to good people. My heart was breaking. How could I answer this? Was there an answer? I had asked this very question myself. I did not know why this happened. Why do bad things happen? Why my son? I was searching for answers. We all were. I didn't know what to say. This was new territory. As parents, you are never prepared to deal with all the curve balls that are thrown at you. At least I wasn't. I had to rely on my instincts and my faith. That was all I had to hold on to at this point. I didn't want to let my son know how scared I was, how uncertain all of these treatments and protocols were. Billy was the first patient at this hospital suffering from this rare disease, and everything was experimental at this point.

After a moment, I simply reassured him that he was a good person, indeed. He had touched so many lives, and so many people loved him and were praying for him. I told him we had to look for the good things that happen. As a matter of fact, he was lucky that the doctors found the tumor when they did. We were told that had it gone undetected much longer, he might not have survived. I don't know if I actually answered his questions or if he was really looking for an answer. I continued with, "All we can hope for at this point is for God to be with us, guiding us day by day." We needed to believe that this was all part of the master plan and that we would get through this ordeal. I promised him he would never be alone. I would always be there for him; I couldn't stress that enough. I don't remember how many times I told him that. I reminded him of all the people who were rooting for him and how we could count on them for support. It goes without saying that we shared a lot of tears. Here was my eighteen-year old son facing an illness that was so horrid. He had been cut open from sternum to pelvis and had an ostomy bag to deal with in addition to catheters, IV ports, pelvic drains, and NG tubes.

To this day, I can still see him looking at me with those beautiful, brown eyes and asking why. I held him in my arms and asked him to be strong. I reminded him of how he had always been there for me. He had always been strong for me when things were down, and now I needed him to stay strong and fight.

Before he had to start the chemotherapy treatments, Billy was trying to get back to a somewhat normal routine. Though he wasn't quite strong enough to go back to work, he did make an effort to go the stone yard a few days a week and assist some of the drivers with installing their plows. There were even a few new drivers who weren't quite sure how to install the plows, so Billy was proud to instruct them. It gave him a sense of pride to still be able to help out somehow and to participate in any capacity at the stone yard. He had a sense of purpose, and it was a good distraction for him.

It was nearing the middle of November, and the plows were installed in preparation of the impending winter snow. This was Billy's favorite season. Every winter he waited in anticipation for that big storm. It was such a rush for him to challenge the elements and plow, either with the trucks or an all-terrain four-wheeler equipped with a snowplow. Since the surgery, he was no longer able to manipulate the manual shovel, but he didn't mind because it was much warmer inside the trucks. There were a few times when he wasn't even able to go out in the trucks, but he would contribute by manning the office and dispatching. On a few occasions, he would bring his brothers along to help. They were always pleased to go with Billy, not just for the company, but they too liked the extra money they were able to earn. The hours were long indeed, and the work was hard, but the money was always an added incentive for them.

We met with Dr. Michaels on November 13 to review our next plan of action. We were given a list of precautions to follow to ensure a bacteria-free environment for Billy. The particular type of medication to be administered was extremely harmful to the cells, and Billy would be at great risk for infection. Dr. Michaels suggested that everyone in the family get the flu shot, and we had to remove everything in the house that would attract or harbor bacteria such as flowers, plants, and fresh fruit and vegetables. Before Billy could undergo a round of chemo, he had to make an appointment with the dentist. Dr. Michaels didn't want to take any chances with the bacteria that forms around the teeth. Lucky I had my notebook with me, as there were so many details and steps to follow before we could even begin the treatment. Billy needed another CT scan so the doctors could start with a baseline study. They were also going to administer a spiral scan of the chest, abdomen, and pelvis. The treatment would consist of high doses of a medicine, Cytoxan, administered intravenously, and required a two-day hospital admission.

We spent the next few weeks preparing for the first stage of the protocol. Billy completed the tasks of having his teeth cleaned, getting his flu shot, and, of course, he had to have the spiral CT baseline scan, which required him to drink the barium mixture. That formula always made him sick and banished his appetite for a day or two. After the effects of the scan, he was able to maintain a healthy diet and exercise routine. He was really starting to feel pretty good. In fact, at his follow-up appointment with the surgeon, he surprised the doctors with how well he was healing. Dr. Berber gave Billy the all clear and told him he didn't have to go back to see her until six to eight weeks after the last round of chemotherapy treatments. It was at that time when Dr. Berber discussed the pros and cons of sperm banking and the options available for Billy, which he declined after serious thought. Another of Dr. Berber's associates also met with Billy that afternoon, and he explained in further detail the protocol and statistics of its success rate. That conversation was as upsetting for Billy, as was the sperm banking. By the time we were home again, he was not only exhausted from the doctor visits, but he was quite depressed. We spent a good part of the evening talking about the trauma he had already been through and the anxiety of what was to come with the treatments. Not knowing whether he could ever reproduce, whether the opportunity arose or not, if he should make it through this, was another question weighing heavily on his mind. Neither of us could come to terms why he was stricken with this, nor could we find reasoning in the suffering. More than anything, I wished I could take the pain from my son. If only I could. I can't remember when I ever felt so totally helpless. I was unable to find any words to allay our fears that night.

One of the most common side effects of chemotherapy was low blood counts, thus wreaking havoc on the immune system. Billy would be extremely susceptible to any type of bacteria or virus that might be lurking about. Knowing this, I immediately contacted someone to clean out the heating ducts in the house while I removed all houseplants. With the help of my mother, we tried as best we could to disinfect the house from top to bottom. If there was the slightest possibility of anything in Billy's environment to be suspect of harm, I was going to do my very best to prevent it. Deep down, I knew I had no control over his illness, but I was going to try my best to control his environment.

When I took the younger boys to the pediatrician's office for their flu shots, we were greeted by a concerned staff. Immediately at the onset of Billy's diagnosis, I sent our pediatricians the literature I had obtained regarding the DSRCT. I thought it was extremely important to have as many medical professionals in the area aware of the signs and symptoms of this disease in the hopes of a prompt diagnosis for future patients, so I faxed literature to them. After all, it took us several months and quite a few doctors to determine the cause of Billy's illness, and in just about all of the cases published, there were misdiagnoses. If education and awareness could help save one person, I was determined to do what I could to help. The staff at our pediatrician's office was so appreciative of the information and data I sent them. They even requested copies of Billy's operative and pathology reports to keep in their files.

Billy wanted to continue his preoperative lifestyle whenever possible. If he had a good night's sleep and was not feeling nauseous, he would look forward to going to work. He would just take it on a day-to-day basis. On the days he went to work, I too would go to the office for a few hours. The firm continued to support my flexible schedule and was willing to work with me.

By this time, we were both starting to become masters of the TPN pump. We were able to customize the cycles to accommodate any late-night plans Billy had. He was supplied with a backpack to house the TPN for outside activities, but Billy was not comfortable traveling with it. We were successful in maintaining his daily intake of TPN with a few minor adjustments, so the backpack wasn't needed. I knew how important it was for Billy to feel as normal as possible and not attract attention. We both tried to get back to a routine, knowing it would only be temporary until the chemotherapy started. Dr. Michaels's office had printed the instructions for the first round of chemotherapy for us. This first stage called for a three-day treatment cycle, which consisted of three drugs—Cytoxan, Adriamycin, and vincristine. Due to the extremely high doses of these drugs, it was required that Billy remain in the hospital for the duration of the infusions. He wasn't at all happy about that fact. He thought maybe he would get the medicine through his IV line and be able to go home, but that wasn't an option, so he prepared himself for a three-day hospital stay.

The closer Billy got to his admission date, the more nauseous he got. The Zofran was no longer working, and he wasn't able to keep anything down. It seemed as though we were calling the doctor every day, and Billy was getting tired of being sick. Even though he was healing nicely from the laparotomy, he still couldn't stop the nausea. Billy felt as though he couldn't get a break. He was aware of the fact that the chemotherapy would make him nauseous, but he was nauseous before he even started the chemo. He couldn't imagine how much worse his symptoms would get then. His frustration and depression were starting to get the best of him. He had a short reprieve of all his symptoms, and now that he was cleared for the chemotherapy, the symptoms of nausea returned; this was beginning to become a constant battle with him. The doctors couldn't figure out why he was so nauseous all the time. They ran a series of tests and were confident there wasn't any blockage in the intestines, and the digestive system appeared to be functioning normally.

The First Infusion

On November 24, 1997, Billy reported to the hospital for his first round of chemotherapy. It took us a lot longer than usual to get to the hospital. We ran into the morning rush-hour traffic, and Billy was extremely nauseous the duration of the ride. I didn't even have time to park the car. I drove immediately to the valet parking area, and Billy exited the car the minute it stopped. I quickly got out of the car and ran over to the other side of the car where Billy was stooped over, vomiting. I shielded him from public view, trying to limit his embarrassment. This was so humiliating for Billy, and he was tired of it. My heart just broke. There was absolutely nothing I could do for him. When he was able, we proceeded to the admissions office, where Billy was assigned to a private room.

Billy reluctantly got in the wheelchair so transportation could take him to the room. Though he preferred to walk, he conceded to the wheelchair due to the nausea. We were greeted by a nurse on the third floor, and I told her about Billy's nausea and vomiting. She was quick to call Dr. Michaels's office to see if they could administer something immediately to stop the nausea, as they wanted to get started with the chemotherapy. Dr. Michaels and a new fellow on staff examined Billy and ordered an obstruction series from X-ray. Dr. Michaels was concerned about the vomiting and thought it best to hold off on the chemotherapy for one day. Billy was beginning to feel a little relief from the nausea once he was hooked up to the IV medicine. They decided to try Kytril for the nausea since the Zofran was ineffective. Billy was both disappointed and discouraged, as he didn't want to delay the start of this treatment. He was counting on being in the hospital for three days and not a day longer.

When Billy returned from the obstruction series, a few more medical students found their way to his room and began questioning Billy about his symptoms and the details of his surgery. By now Billy was getting accustomed to these queries, and in addition to being ready with his answers, he also provided them with printed information we had copied from the Internet. Most of these students, as well as the doctors, were not at all familiar with DSRCT. The printed literature was greatly appreciated, besides saving both Billy and me a lot of time describing this rare tumor to them.

Surprisingly, Billy had another decent night. I guess it was all the IV medicines they gave him. The nurses told him it was his bedtime cocktail—Kytril, Ativan, and Decadron. This indeed made him drowsy, and he slept through the night. Dr. Berber was assigned the afternoon rounds the next day, and she was pleased Billy was finally sustaining some nutrition through his meals rather than depending on the TPN. She told us that as soon as Dr. Michaels examined Billy and gave him the all clear, they would start the chemotherapy. Billy was beginning to get impatient by this time. He had already lost a day due to the nausea, and he was counting on getting home in precisely three days.

Initially the chemotherapy was scheduled to commence on Monday; it was already Wednesday, and they had not yet started the chemotherapy. The doctors were waiting for the specific gravity numbers to come back from the lab. The dosage of medication they planned to use was harmful to the bladder, and they had to be extremely careful not to cause any damage to it. Unfortunately for Billy, the chemotherapy was delayed for three days, and by this time we were really cutting it close to the fundraising benefit our community of friends were hosting for Billy on Saturday. By that time, it also meant we would have had to spend Thanksgiving in the hospital. Billy was disappointed that he wasn't able to spend the holiday at his grandmother's house along with his siblings— Nicole, Matthew, and Sean—aunts, uncles, and cousins, though they did bring us a platter. Later in the evening of the holiday, Billy's spirits were lifted, as his friends Kevin, Jeremy, and Matt came to visit him. I knew how happy Billy was when he was with his friends. I decided to go to the lounge for a while so they could have a private visit without Mom around. It was great to see Billy interact with his friends, and I knew how much he appreciated the time they spent with him.

With the delay in starting the chemo, it was apparent that Billy would be in the hospital until the day of the benefit, and there was nothing we could do about that. Dr. Michaels went over in detail the side effects of each drug they would be using and the precautions they had to take to protect the bladder, kidneys, and liver. There were many dangers associated with each of these drugs, and they had severe contraindications. Billy's surgeon was kind enough to give me printed literature on each of the medicines they would be using during phase one of the protocol. It was confusing to keep track of all these medications, but I wanted all the information I could possibly have concerning his care and treatment. Each drug was administered via injection and in a specific sequence.

Days one and two, Billy was given a drug called Cytoxan, which ran over a period of six hours each day. They also had to administer Lasix, a diuretic to flush the deadly chemicals out of his system. Dr. Michaels explained that it was necessary for them to begin a separate IV for the Lasix, as they had to flush the drug out of his system as quickly as possible, and they had to monitor his urine output closely. He needed to put out one hundred cc's every forty-five minutes. The next drug used was Adriamycin, which was infused on all three days of phase one. This drug ran continuously on a slow drip over a twenty-four-hour period for less chance of problems. The third drug was vincristine, which also ran continuously for the three days. We were again reminded of the high risk for bacteria and that some of the side effects included mouth sores, hair loss, and, of course, nausea. Billy had to be given another drug, mesna, which also had to run over twenty-four hours to protect his bladder. The mesna did not mix with the Lasix or the vincristine, but the Lasix had to run the full six hours the Cytoxan ran. Due to the sensitivity of each of these drugs and the specific sequences they had to run, Billy and I kept a very close eye on each bag as it was hung on his pole. The next two days, the chemo ran its course, and Billy tolerated it as well as could be expected. As usual, Billy wasn't able to sleep through the night. The Lasix was running its course, and Billy was voiding almost continuously. Even though he had a catheter, the staff was in his room every hour, measuring his output and emptying the canisters. Anyone who has ever been in the hospital knows that no matter how quiet the staff tries to be, the light shines through the door the minute it is opened, and the running water seems to echo louder at night. It was difficult to get a good night's sleep for either of us. But we persevered, and we were able to go home on Saturday, just in time for the benefit.

We were given a list of discharge instructions, and it was especially important that Billy brush his teeth several times a day with a peroxide solution using a soft-bristled brush and a baking soda rinse. The doctors wanted Billy to drink plenty of milkshakes and maintain a high-calorie, nutritious diet, but, ironically, he had to stay away from fresh fruits and vegetables due to the exposure to bacteria. We were told to expect a big drop in Billy's blood cell counts around the seventh day after chemo. For this reason, I had to be taught how to give injections (Dr. Michaels referred to them as GCSF). Billy had to get Neupogen and Epogen injections when his red and white blood counts were low, and I had to learn how to give them. As stated earlier, I had no nursing background and was always squeamish when it came to anything beyond basic first-aid care, but I had to learn quickly how to care for my son.

Angels of Mercy

B illy was a young man beyond his years and had touched the hearts of many people. This was evident by the large turnout at the party. We were overwhelmed at the size of the crowd. Everyone cheered when Billy entered the room; it brought tears to my eyes. As Billy tried to make his way through the room to greet each guest individually, he too was overcome with emotion. As happy as he was to be surrounded by so many people who loved him and cared about him, the previous three days of intense chemotherapy played havoc on his body as well as his mind, and he was completely drained. Shortly after we arrived, Monsignor Alleyne blessed the food, and everyone enjoyed the buffet. After dinner the dancing began, and everyone got teary eyed when Billy danced with his sister. It was one of the most beautiful memories for Nicole. Though we were only able to stay about two hours, I do believe everyone enjoyed themselves and was glad they didn't miss the event. This was Billy's night, a night where the community so proudly paid tribute to him.

Many people donated both their time and their services, including the caterer, DJ, Chinese Auction committee, ticket committee, local retailers, and politicians, each willing to share so much of themselves, making generous contributions and more importantly, providing an abundance of emotional support. Our hearts were touched beyond measure, and I can only hope my words of thanks expressed our deepest gratitude and appreciation. We had been touched by many angels. The kindness and generosity did not stop at the benefit. We continued to receive an endless supply of groceries and prayers from many surrounding communities and parishes. My coworkers even sponsored a raffle on Billy's behalf, the proceeds of which were delivered to our home the day before Thanksgiving. We had a lot to be thankful for and everyone's generosity was quite overwhelming. Just a few days later, when the committee completed their paperwork, I was given a list of participants and their addresses. I sent each of them a thank-you and hoped I could truly express our gratitude for all they had done. I tried my best to recount our appreciation and thankfulness.

The couple of days following the benefit, Billy again tried to regain some of his strength. Kevin went to the house often, and the two of them would watch movies. Many times, Kevin would spend the night; he was truly a dedicated friend, and I know how much it meant to Billy. Having Kevin around boosted Billy's spirits so much. Sometimes I would hear them as they would carry on and watch movies or play video games like the old days. Billy knew Kevin could have been out with other friends, but he chose to stay with Billy. I must emphasize how much his friendship meant.

Billy's strength and stamina, as well as good cell counts, didn't last too long, however. Just as we were told, his counts were their lowest from day eight to day fourteen, so I had to give him the GCSF injections during that week. Since Billy was weak from the chemotherapy, he had to have many high-calorie snacks between meals. Dr. Michaels recommended milkshakes after his meals and as much custard, pudding, peanut butter crackers, etc., to keep up his strength because he was scheduled to have the second round of chemotherapy nineteen days after the first round (December 15, 1997). The effects of the chemo were as bad as we were told. Billy's immune system was compromised, he did come down with a bladder infection and had to be hospitalized overnight.

Once the counts began to increase, so did Billy's strength. On the night before his second chemo admission, Kevin took Billy to the Flyers game. Billy was able to make it through the entire game and was so glad he went. He enjoyed it so much he commented that he would like to try to get tickets for another game. I was happy he was able to get to enjoy the game too. It gave him something nice to think about while he was in the hospital the next few days.

Round Two

As scheduled, Billy and I arrived at the hospital on December 15, 1997, for the second round of chemo. We were brought to his room around eight thirty in the morning, but they didn't start the pre-chemo meds (Lasix, potassium) until about two p.m. At four fifteen in the afternoon, they started the Cytoxan, Adriamycin, and vincristine. That first day wasn't too bad for Billy, and he still had an appetite. He was able to enjoy his visit with Aunt JoAnne and Josh, and he even asked for snacks. After his visitors left, we were both tired. We tried to go to bed early but waited until the nurse started his TPN at eleven fifteen. We had a decent night's rest; only up a few times. The nurse did have to change the bed linens around two forty-five a.m., and Billy was embarrassed about that, but the nurse was great; she explained this was not unusual with that type of medication. She also explained that the chemotherapy was toxic, thereby making the body's secretion and fluids toxic, and we had to be especially careful when handling them. The hospital linens were disposed of in the toxic waste containers provided, and I rinsed his personal clothing in the shower before bagging them for home. The important thing was to remove the toxins from his skin as soon as possible and for me to wear gloves.

On the second day of round two, Dr. Torpy and Rocco, the fellow resident, examined Billy and told him he had to try to eat a little more in order to keep up his strength. One of his labs showed a trace of bacteria in his urine again, but they thought it might have been due to the stents. His blood sugar was over three hundred, and he had to have an insulin injection. We were told TPN was to blame for the high sugar count, so they suspended the TPN while he was in the hospital. Dr. Michaels didn't see Billy until after dinner, and she reminded him he was at a high-metabolic stage and should take four multivitamins daily. She told me that once we were home, I would have to administer an injection called Epogen, which was used to boost the red blood cells.

Later that afternoon, Billy's labs showed he needed a blood transfusion, which he was told was also normal after chemo-therapy. He was a bit concerned about receiving blood products due to all the negative results and diseases associated with blood transfusions. Dr. Parks, a fourth-year medical student, was kind enough to spend some time with Billy, explaining the pros and cons of a transfusion, and he told Billy it was a valid concern to think about hepatitis and the HIV virus with transfusions. He said the chances were less than one in one hundred thousand, and if it were him, there'd be no question, he would get the blood, as it would make him feel a lot better. Billy's hemoglobin was barely at eight, and they wanted it to be at least twelve. It was at that point that I decided to start getting copies of all Billy's lab reports. I wanted to keep my own records to review and compare. The doctors and nurses were more than compliant, and I began receiving copies of every lab report, test, and procedure from that time on. At midnight, Billy's blood sugars were up again, and he was given another insulin injection. Unfortunately, he did not get much sleep that second night, as he was up frequently to go to the bathroom.

On December 17, Dr. Michaels and Dr. Torpy both went into Billy's room after their rounds to go over the process for the bone marrow transplant. Since the chemotherapy depresses the red and white cells, it was planned that we collect the stem cells prior to the third treatment. If everything else stayed on course and there were no signs of infection, we were to be discharged on the eighteenth of the month. Dr. Michaels's office would have someone from a Dr. Bard's office call me for an appointment, and I would get further instructions regarding the stem cell collection. In the meantime, I had started administering the Neupogen injections on Saturday, and the Epogen was to start on the twenty-fourth.

By this time, Billy and I had spent much time at the hospital and were beginning to form new friendships with some of the nursing staff. There was one particular nurse, Ann, who paid extra attention to us during our hospital stays. She was especially fond of Billy, and they had a great rapport. One day while I was at the office, Ann visited Billy in his room. In his words, "She said she knew they were always joking and had fun on their visits, but she wanted to get serious for a while. She was curious as to how he was coping with all of this. She explained that she could only imagine how difficult it had to be for him to deal with all of this. In addition to recovering from a very serious surgery, he also had to muster up the courage to deal with a life-threatening illness. This would be difficult for anyone, but one could only imagine the emotional and mental stress it would have on such a young man of eighteen. She told him that if he ever, ever needed to talk, she would be there for him. She may not have all the answers, but he could count on her support."

There were so many little angels of mercy watching over us, and, as a mother, I was especially touched at the kindness and concern of this nurse, as so many other nurses' kindness. Their compassion and true concern for this patient, my son, was commendable. There were, however, a few nurses who never should have chosen the nursing profession. One incident in particular involved a nurse, by the name of Madonna who was always disgruntled and rude, that I had found the need to make a formal complaint. I really don't know what they did about her, and I really don't care, but I do know that she was never assigned to Billy on any further admissions. Billy was so easy to get along with and so well liked by the staff. The younger staff members, orderlies, and nursing assistants would always stop by to see him if they knew he was at the hospital. Sometimes we would get visits from nurses on other floors once they found out he was in the hospital. They must have randomly checked the computer or something. There were days when he was not feeling well and he wasn't very sociable, but he was never rude and never did anything to provoke or deserve negative treatment by anyone. But, again, they were far and few between.

There was another nurse we encountered on one of our visits to Jefferson whom I found to be a bit standoffish and not very sociable. She was pleasant enough when she tended to Billy, but she always appeared to be in a hurry to leave the room. On one particular evening, however, Billy was having a reaction to his meds, and the doctors needed to run a few tests to rule out an infection or a blockage. During testing, I was pacing the halls and I was approached by that nurse who nervously explained that she had a son Billy's age and found it difficult to see my son lying there, sick in bed, coping with this dreaded disease. She was overcome with empathy and compassion but found it too difficult to face. She didn't want Billy to think she was pitying him and was afraid she would break down in tears, so she tried to keep it totally professional, focusing on her duties and avoiding any small talk. It was eating away at her, and she didn't want me to think her aloof approach to my son would in any way interfere with his care. She wished me well and continued on to the nurses' station. I was dumbfounded by her candor; not knowing what to say, I simply smiled and thanked her.

blood samples. Billy's white blood cell counts were 69,000, and his platelets were 257,000. The collection went a little faster on the second day, and we were able to go home for lunch. The reports were sent immediately to Dr. Michaels's office and she called me to start the heparin flushes again in the morning. Taking advantage of the extra daylight hours, I decided to go to the office for a few hours while Billy enjoyed the unseasonably mild weather and installed new rims on his car and then went to the carwash. After dinner he was starting to feel nauseous and weak, so he decided to make it an early night; he and Kevin stayed in and watched a movie.

Medicine Man was our movie of choice during the third and final day of the collection. We sat comfortably and enjoyed the matinee and snacks. Billy was anxious to finish and hopeful that he gave a good collection. His white blood cells on that third day were 81,900, and his platelets were 190,000. Someone from Jefferson bone marrow transplant unit called us while we were still at the Red Cross and said Billy had a beautiful collection and they were pleased with his progress. Billy looked relieved with the news, and we were both even more excited when they told us it looked as if we would have extra cells.

By the end of that collection cycle, Billy was overcome with nausea, so we waited a while before going home. Ryan was at the house by the time we got there, and he was concerned with Billy's nausea and the fact he was showing signs of edema. He made a note of it on the chart and had me call Dr. Michaels's office, who wanted to see us immediately. Billy wasn't too pleased with me when I told him we had to go to the doctor. He was looking forward to curling up in his own bed and getting some rest. I knew he was tired, but at the same time, I didn't want to take any chances with infection or anything. Fortunately, our doctor's visit showed no infection, but his potassium levels were low, and this was something we could remedy without having to admit Billy.

January 8, 1998, we had another regularly scheduled appointment with Dr. Michaels, and while waiting for the results of the day's lab work, Janet from the bone marrow transplant unit stopped by to see Billy and removed his port while we were in the office. Billy was a bit shocked when she removed it right then and there. She took him by surprise, and he wasn't at all comfortable being probed and plucked without warning or notice. On the other hand, however, we were both grateful we didn't have to return to the city on another visit just to have the port removed.

Billy had a few questions for Dr. Michaels concerning the puffiness and weight gain he was experiencing. Dr Michaels told him it was a result of the steroids and once they weaned him from them, he would start to lose some of the puffiness. It was a bit unusual to see Billy with a few extra pounds. Regardless, he was beginning to feel stronger, and his appetite was returning, and that was a big improvement. We weren't sure how long that would last, though, because he was due to begin the third round of chemo the following Monday.

ing him how sorry I was that this had to be done. I explained to him that it was necessary to get to the bottom of the vomiting. He couldn't survive if he continued to vomit constantly, and there were certain things we had to let the doctors do that were not pleasant but necessary for a diagnosis and a cause. The resident brought him lidocaine to numb his throat, and after the tube was in for fifteen to twenty minutes, a large amount of bloody discharge filled the tube. At six thirty that same evening, February 2, 1998, after being in the hospital since five thirty in the morning, Dr. Felix (Joanne) who introduced herself as Joanne, was the doctor on call for the weekend, who eventually became a wonderful friend to Billy. She was sympathetic to his anxiety and displeasure with the tube but expressed she could not yet remove it. She informed us that Drs. Michaels and Berber were on their rounds, and we she would alert them of his discomfort. As it turned out, we didn't see either of them until much later in the evening. When Dr. Michaels finally went in to see Billy, he was agitated that the NG tube was in and he was still vomiting and adamant he wanted it out immediately. She promised to take the NG tube out that night, provided she could get the CT scan done. Several hours later, when Dr. Michaels called down to nuclear medicine to see what the delay was in obtaining the CT scan, she was told Billy wasn't on the schedule until morning. Needless to say, since there was no CT scan done, the NG tube was in another night.

Billy continued to vomit throughout the night and into the next morning. The nurse gave him IV Ativan to help him sleep, and they ran another IV line with potassium. Just as he was beginning to fall asleep at 4:30 a.m., the nurse disturbed him for vital signs. He returned to a somewhat comfortable position when he was interrupted once again at 7:00 a.m. for those vitals. Around ten o'clock in the morning on February 3, Billy was presented with a quart-sized bottle of barium solution for the CT scan, which was to be administered through the NG tube. Despite his emphatic protests to forego the barium contrast, his objections were overruled, and he was instructed to begin immediately, followed by another dose at eleven thirty.

The NG tube provided no purpose at this point, as Billy continued to vomit the barium as quickly as it was consumed. At his request, I immediately called Dr. Michaels's office and requested an immediate consult, but instead Dr. Flander entered the room to assess the situation. She acknowledged Billy's discomfort and flushed the NG tube. Satisfied that they were able to bring up almost all of the barium left in the stomach, Dr. Berber agreed not to administer the second dose of the solution. Transportation clumsily crashed into the room around 12:45 p.m. to bring him down to nuclear medicine for the test.

As of three o'clock, we still had not received any test results, and Billy continued to request removal of the NG tube. He was insistent to get his way, and together we sat and prayed a novena to Padre Pio. Dr. Michaels did not enter Billy's room until seven fifteen that evening, and we were quite aggravated by her lackadaisical attitude. Unfortunately, removal of the NG tube was not an option at this time. The gastroenterologist examined Billy and immediately scheduled him for an endoscopy the following day. They increased his IV dosage of Zantac in an effort to remove the stomach acid. If the endoscopy didn't show anything, then they had to do a lower GI series. The doctor assured us that he would get to the bottom of the nausea and vomiting, as it had gone on long enough. In addition to the nausea and vomiting, Billy's hemoglobin counts were extremely low, and the doctors were talking of another blood transfusion possibly in the morning. Billy's dad wanted to donate blood for Billy, but we were advised it would take two to three days at Jefferson to process, and Billy needed the blood then. We were told the blood was only kept two to three weeks, and the donor cannot give blood again for five to six months. Had we known then how much blood Billy would have needed, we would have given it at that time and again in five to six months as well. It certainly would not have gone to waste.

Billy signed the release for the transfusion then asked the doctor if he would remove the NG tube again. With disdain in his eyes, Billy looked at the doctor as he explained to him why it would not be a good idea to remove the tube prematurely but promised he would present it to Dr. Michaels and wait for her advisement. Billy's next round of chemotherapy was still on hold, and the CT scans were pending, so we had to wait in limbo for answers.

Needless to say, it wasn't the best of nights, but Billy was able to get some uninterrupted sleep, at least two hours at a time. By seven thirty the next morning, another doctor examined Billy and explained the endoscopy procedure and what they were looking for. The procedure itself was scheduled for nine o'clock, and the actual testing time was about forty-five minutes. By eight forty-five in the morning, transport was in Billy's room with the stretcher, right on schedule. They allowed me to go as far as the holding area, where I was left behind closed doors in a room with a few gray leather chairs. I repeated the novena to Padre Pio while waiting patiently for the doctor to come out and speak with me. At ten o'clock, I saw the gastroenterologist walking toward me. He said Billy was just brought to the holding area and they didn't find anything "too bad," but there was quite a lot of gastritis, all of which was caused by irritation of the NG tube, the chemotherapy, and vomiting. The plan was to continue him on strong doses of chemotherapy. The doctor also advised us that there was not too much fluid in the stomach. Billy had developed a moderate case of esophagitis, burning all up the esophagus. He was prescribed high doses of Zantac, which was gradually tapered off, and then a regimen of Prilosec was started. If the vomiting continued, then Billy had to drink the barium and have them check the lower end of the bowel. He was kept on fluids for a few hours and then observed over the next forty-eight hours with Zantac. After the procedure, they removed the NG tube. Finally!

The next day, Dr. Michaels went in and was happy to report that Billy's hemoglobin counts were back up to ten, and if he continued to keep fluids down and try light foods, he could possibly go home the following day. Billy was thrilled, and so was I. He felt he would be more comfortable at home and just wanted to get back to some sort of routine. Just having the NG tube removed gave him so much relief. We tried the liquid diet. Nicole brought him chicken noodle soup, and he was able to keep it down. The kitchen sent up Jell-O and broth for his lunch, which he managed to keep the Jell-O down. His stomach was feeling full quickly, so we didn't want to push it. He took it slow and ate one or two teaspoons at a time. He drank his liquids slowly over a period of about an hour and ate Jell-O and broth just as slowly.

Dr. Michaels suggested that Billy's head be elevated while he ate, as when lying flat, the esophagus tends to move food and acid up. She also told him she didn't want him to get anxious or nervous. That was a difficult assignment. Billy was already anxious, just being in the hospital and going through all these procedures. It was difficult to keep him from getting nervous. Heck, I was nervous too. How do you stay calm when you are lying in a hospital bed? Regardless, we tried to keep his mind on other things, and I suggested he do some painting or work on a model he had in his closet. His cousin Joshua brought Billy his Game Boy, and Billy did enjoy playing video games, so he was content with that. Later, I had Nicole bring my notebook computer from home. It had some card games that Billy enjoyed playing. We tried to give him as many activities as possible to keep him occupied.

Since Billy was doing so well and keeping down the liquids, the doctors agreed to discharge Billy. I was confident he was going home that day. Earlier that morning I had received another call from Father Sylvester, a Capuchin priest and very dear friend of the family. It was always wonderful to hear from him. He is such a spiritual man; sometimes I would get chills through the phone when he speaks. He said he was continuing to pray to Padre Pio with us and for us. He wanted to be kept informed of Billy's progress, and, of course, he asked for our prayers as well. He was going on a retreat, which was probably his last, due to his health. And then he blessed us over the phone. I told Billy about the call as soon as I arrived at the hospital, hoping it would ease his anxiety.

From the moment Billy awoke, he waited for the discharge papers. As the morning progressed and still no word from the doctor, Billy started to get perturbed. I asked the nurse for the blood count report, and she kindly got a copy for me; the numbers looked good. I just assured Billy that the doctors would be in soon and it was probably better that he stayed through lunch to make sure he was able to keep the food down. I reminded him of Father Sylvester's phone call. I told him he would be going home and not to worry. "I can almost guarantee it," I said. We both agreed that it would be worse to go home and find he couldn't handle eating and then have to come back to the hospital. Shortly after we finished another prayer to Padre Pio and recited the Our Father together, Dr. Flander entered the room with a smile.

After announcing that Billy was good to go, we listened to the list of discharge instructions. Billy was to take Prilosec three times a day, and we needed to be diligent about any problems with food, fever, or discomfort. If Billy began to experience any problems or difficulties, we were to call the hospital immediately. They didn't want anything to get too far. Dr. Flander already informed us that the urinalysis report had come back showing signs of infection, and Billy had to continue with the Cipro and Bactrim, unless anything else cropped its little head up and needed attention. Dr. Michaels also stopped by to see Billy and suggested we added a little Mylanta or Maalox to his diet to help coat the stomach. She asked that he try to stay away from spicy foods and caffeine. Billy didn't really consume much caffeine other than an occasional soda or iced tea, but we were able to adjust for that. He was just anxious to get home and be in his own environment once again.

By this time, I was anxious to get out of the hospital as well, but I was still waiting for a CT scan report from Dr. Michaels. She said her assistant had gone down to get me a copy. They all knew I was documenting every test and scan personally, and somehow I never received a copy of this one. I was particularly interested in this scan. I wanted to see it in writing. The results were read to us, and when we heard them, Billy and I had tears in our eyes and hugged each other. The tumor on the spleen had completely resolved, and the tumor on the pari-aorta had resolved. The tumors on the liver had substantially decreased. There was no mention of the diaphragm at all on this test, and we figured maybe it just wasn't addressed as part of the scan. The lung bases were clear, and there was no evidence of metastasis to the bones.

"Thank You, sweet Jesus. Thank You," I cried with joy. Another doctor who happened to be in the next room heard all the excitement, so he went in to Billy's room to acknowledge the good news as well. Everyone was extremely pleased with Billy's progress. It was evident that our prayers to Padre Pio and every other angel in heaven were working overtime on Billy's behalf. When Dr. Michaels finally went into the room, she was smiling, as she knew we had just been given the good news of the CT scan, and she also confirmed the pre-certification from Dr. DiMarcangelo's office for Monday's chemotherapy. As soon as the discharge papers were signed, we gathered our things and headed for home. Needless to say, Billy and I went home very happy that day.

The next few days went well for Billy, and he was able to enjoy Kevin's company without being sick. They went out for a few hours in the afternoon, and when he got tired, Billy would go home and watch movies with Matthew and Sean while catching

Round Four

In February of 1998, the MRI suggested that multiple small left-lung base nodules greater on the right than on the left might represent transdiaphragmatic spread, as well as small para-aortic lymph nodes. There was evidence of iron overload in the spleen and in the liver, which was most likely secondary to the multiple transfusions, hemosiderosis. My chest tightened as I read along the printed lines of the report. My facial expression reflected confusion and fear, but the doctor's reaction was quite to the contrary. He indicated that he was pleased with the findings of the report. Although there were few new nodules, he reassured me there was a decrease in the size of the right anterior lymph node. He further explained that the previously seen dominant right basilar lung nodule was not visible on that examination, nor did he see a previous visible subpleural nodule on the left lateral lung base. His calm demeanor had no effect on me. It was obvious the doctor saw the glass as half full, yet all I could see was how empty it was getting. In my eyes, these MRI findings described new suspicious small round growths that I felt were immediate red flags. This report was certainly very different from the CT scan we received a month ago. What changed since then?

I didn't want to be pessimistic, but nothing in this report gave me comfort. Of course, when I relayed the findings to Billy, I did take the doctor's lead and focused on the nodes that had indeed decreased in size. Billy just looked into my eyes and tried to get a read on what I was feeling. I couldn't lie to him, nor could I disappoint him. I tried my hardest to convince the two of us that the doctor's words were reassuring and there was some improvement. I'm not sure whether the doctor was genuinely satisfied with this report or if he was simply relieved the findings weren't worse, and I'll probably never know. I had to hang on to my faith. Billy and I continued our novena to Padre Pio, and he appreciated every moment spent together with family and friends.

We began round four of the P6 protocol on February 9, 1998. Billy's blood sugars were low, so they waited a few hours to take another sample. By the time Dr. Michaels arrived at Billy's room, it was seven fifteen at night, and she still didn't have the chemotherapy orders signed. She told us we weren't able to administer the medication because Billy's urine was too concentrated. We were told the levels should be no higher than 1010, and his were coming in at 1020. Upset with yet another delay in starting the chemotherapy, Billy withdrew into a long silence and shook his head.

He was appeased, however, when the nurse suggested they start the IV fluids as soon as possible in an attempt to correct his deficiencies. They ran twenty milligrams of fucosemide, one thousand milligrams of dextrose, and twenty milligrams of potassium chloride.

Billy and I watched the Olympics and then fell fast asleep. Billy woke up a couple of times during the night, as the liquids were going right through him. He felt bad waking me, but I told him that's what I was there for. The purpose of the fluids was to flush his system, and it was necessary for him to let nature run its course. By five fifteen in the morning, we were up again, and that time we had to change the linens and nightclothes. Neither Billy nor I could go back to sleep. Breakfast came close to eight o'clock that day, and the day nurse went over the specifics of the protocol with us. She said this course of chemo shouldn't make him as sick as the last round. We started the VP-16 at nine in the morning, and it ran for one hour every day for the next five days. The ifosfamide was to run for six hours every day for five consecutive days, and the mesna was to run continuously over a twenty-four-hour period for five days. Although the chemotherapy did not make Billy as sick as the last round, it did make him extremely sleepy. He slept a lot during the next few days. I felt secure with his care, and he was comfortable enough for me to go to the office for a few hours during this round. I would put in a few hours in the morning, spend one-and-a-half hours with him for lunch, and then work a few more hours in the afternoon. On the way back to the hospital, I would occasionally stop at one of the local department stores and purchase a few more sleep pants or comfortable shirts for him to keep as spares. He always appreciated getting a few new things. Nicole was home at that time, so she and her dad would alternate visits to the hospital and home with Matthew and Sean.

Over the next few days, Billy's blood-glucose levels began to reach the two hundred level, and he needed insulin injections. The doctors increased his Lasix in an attempt to flush the medication out of his system quickly, which was precisely what it did. I continued to work a few hours at the office, and Nicole and Bill continued their alternate visits between home and the hospital. One afternoon, Father Sylvester called me at the New Jersey office, and they transferred the call to the Philadelphia office so I could talk to him. It was wonderful to speak with him again. He said he had to call. Billy had been on his mind, and he had a premonition that something good was happening. He said he loved us, and he blessed us, and would continue his prayers to

Padre Pio for us. I was comforted by his phone call and shared it with Billy. He too was comforted, and together we prayed our novena to Padre Pio.

Billy tolerated this round of chemotherapy much better than the previous rounds. He was able to keep food down, able to sleep, and his mood was positive. Whenever Dr. Michaels went in for her patient rounds, she expressed optimism in Billy's progress. She even went so far as to say that she had just sent a summary to Dr. Kushner and the review board, advising how well Billy was handling this round of chemotherapy and the results of the most recent CT scan. It was even suggested that, due to the progress, it might be a consideration to push up the radiation and second surgery, which would eliminate some of the chemotherapy. Her exact words at that time were "He [Billy] has surprised everyone with his response to the chemotherapy, everyone except me."

Billy and I just looked at each other with a grin. We knew it was Father Sylvester. Tears in our eyes, we knew there was hope. We even told Dr. Michaels that it was through the intervention of Padre Pio and the angels that we were receiving this positive response. Billy and I continued our prayers. Despite the positive attitude of the doctors, Billy confided in me that he was a bit apprehensive to alter the P6 protocol and eliminate or postpone some of the chemotherapy. He said he had mixed feelings about it. If the P6 protocol worked, why would we make any changes to it? When we presented this argument to Dr. Michaels, she advised that she was very cautious. She would not alter the proto-col without the advisement of Dr. Kushner and the board. It was just a suggestion, as each case was handled on an individual basis, and the patients each had an opportunity to individualize their treatment based upon their response to the therapy. She further stated that the chemotherapy medications used in the protocol were quite harsh, and if any could be eliminated, it would be to his further benefit, as the chemo, which we knew, had so many side effects and downsides that the less in his system, sometimes the better. We went a little further with our questioning and asked about the specifics of the radiation therapy. Dr. Michaels went over the radiation plans and said at first it would be a general radiation of the entire abdomen, not one specific area. Then I asked if they pushed up the radiation and surgery then needed to do more chemotherapy at a later date, would it be a possibility. She said yes, it certainly would be a possibility and definitely not a problem to have subsequent chemotherapy with GSF (Neupogen), providing we did not exceed the total recommended chemotherapy prescribed. She reminded us at that time the amount of chemotherapy P6 protocol required was the maximum dose of chemotherapy that could possibly be given, and there was no way to ever exceed that amount, but we were free to administer less and, if necessary, add additional chemotherapy up to the amount prescribed.

Other than a few increased blood-sugar counts and occasional insulin injections, Billy continued with his positive response to the treatment. Of course, there were still issues with the Lasix and Billy's urine output. The doctors wanted to make sure he was increasing his fluids in order to flush the harsh chemicals out of his system. During the evening hours, Billy and I would walk through the halls, Billy pulling his IV pole and strolling along talking to the nurses and occasionally stopping at the vending machine for a snack or a ginger ale, and I would review my notes for the day. Some of the nurses would comment on my notebook, asking Billy if I was writing a book. Billy would grin and tell them, "Yeah, you better be careful." We would laugh and continue on our way. It had become a joke with a few of the staff and Billy. Some of them even took it so far as a "made-for-TV-movie." They had the cast selected—Matt Damon to play the part of Billy and Susan Sarandon for his mom.

Billy still had a lot of questions running through his mind, and he wanted me to present them to Dr. Michaels. Specifically, he wanted to know an approximate date when the radiation would

start. Then he was concerned as to why every round of chemotherapy had a warning of the risk of a second cancer occurring
at a later date. Dr. Michaels responded that the occurrence of
a secondary cancer was a possibility at a later date because the
patient was more susceptible to cancer cells due to a compromised immune system once the cells were exposed to the chemicals. She explained that was the reason they kept a close eye on
Billy, especially after the chemotherapy, with routine blood tests
and scans. She offered to bring Billy a copy of a chapter she had
authored regarding side effects and long-term post-tumor/cancer
treatment and care.

Once Billy knew he would be discharged on Sunday, he had
a few more questions for Dr. Michaels concerning his social cal-
endar. First, he wanted to know how he would be feeling by the
twenty-eighth of the month, as his dear friend Dominic was getting married on that date, and he was planning to attend the
wedding. He also gave Dr. Michaels a list of upcoming events,
including both Sean's and Nicole's graduations in May. He
wanted to make sure he was feeling up to par for those events
rather than have chemotherapy or other treatments scheduled
around them, in which he would not be able to participate. Dr.
Michaels assured Billy he would be fine for Dominic and Diane's
wedding, and as far as Sean and Nicole's graduations in May, she
thought it was too early to give him an answer. She did offer,
however, that if he continued to progress as he was, she believed
he would be fine.

A few days before Billy's discharge from the hospital, Matthew
and Sean went to the hospital with Nicole. Matthew slept at the
hospital Friday night with me, and Saturday he went home, as
friends of his, the Schantz boys, had made plans to sleep at our
house just to give the boys a night of fun. Bill was home with
them and said he would be able to supervise. Anyway, we all
knew they needed a few moments of normality too.

By the time we were ready to discuss Billy's discharge home, we had received several e-mails from friends and family stating that they were planning on being in the area the following weekend and wanted to make plans with Billy. He was thrilled. Uncle Bob was planning on coming in, as well as my nephew Jason. He also received a call from his dear friend Jeremy stating that he had a weekend leave from the Navy and would be expected in town that same weekend. Billy was looking forward to seeing Jeremy. It had been months since they last spoke, and he truly enjoyed his company.

Valentine's Day, 1998, was a bit of a somber day for Billy. He was really feeling down and expressed a deep desire to go home. We went for a short walk down the hall then sat outside his hospital room in a small waiting area. We had a profound heart to heart, and both of us shed a few tears. I told Billy how hard I and everyone else were praying for an end to all of his pain and for a complete healing. He said he didn't think he was asking for too much. He just wanted the ileostomy bag to be gone and the port out forever. He repeated again that he just wanted to go home and stay home. When I reminded him of all the positive aspects of the most recent CT scan report and the optimism of his doctors, I also pointed out that it was almost over. Especially if we were able to side step at least one round of the chemotherapy. His instant reply to me was "Mom, almost only counts in hand grenades and horseshoes."

I continued with my narrative of how painful it is for a mother to have this happen to her son. I assured him of how much I loved him and of my confidence and faith that it would soon be behind us. We shed a few more tears, I held him in my arms, and then we headed for dinner. After dinner, we watched the Olympics and tried to get some sleep. Unfortunately, Billy wasn't able to sleep that night. He had to constantly get up to go to the bathroom. His nurse said his urine specimen came back with evidence of a urinary-tract infection. Since they already had him on Cipro two times daily, they said they would just continue with that dosage. His potassium and sodium were low at that time too, and we were advised that Ryan, the home-care nurse, would be checking on those levels again, if and when we finally got home. As of that time, it appeared discharge would possibly be delayed another day or two.

The following day when Dr. Michaels made her rounds, she assured us that all of Billy's labs were beginning to improve, and other than the slight UTI, if everything else continued to progress, she would be able to discharge him the following day. Billy was happy to hear that. There was nothing he would rather do than go home. As promised, Billy was discharged the next day, as his labs continued to progress.

Since he was discharged late on Saturday afternoon, Billy had many visitors awaiting his arrival home. His Aunt JoAnne made the short drive to our house, bringing her youngest son, Anthony, who was especially anxious to see Billy since he wanted Billy to help him with the design and construction of his Home Run Derby car for the Cub Scouts. Billy was thrilled that Anthony asked for his help and immediately suggested a few design ideas and tips on how to integrate the specific wheel and weight require-ments. Billy had participated in the Home Run Derby when he was a Cub Scout, and he helped each of his brothers, Matthew and Sean, with their cars when it was their turn for the derby years earlier. Each of the boys' cars did quite well in their respec-tive races, and Anthony was anxious to finally get the chance to build and race his own car. The following afternoon, after we had all gone to mass, Billy's great-grandmother and Aunt Edith and Godmother Louisa came to our house for dinner, along with Billy's Nan and Grandpop Bob. Everyone was so happy to see Billy in such good spirits, and consequently, no one was in a hurry leave. We sat around the dining room table for hours, just talking and laughing and reminiscing of days past. It was good to see my grandmother in such great spirits. After all, she was ninety-seven years old but she still had a great sense of humor and was quite independent. Grandmom was the matriarch of our family, and everyone always gathered when she was around. She had an aura of warmth and love about her, and the children gravitated toward her charm and were often mesmerized as they listened to her stories of days past. Her tales brought back memories for all of us. It was especially funny to hear antics of her children and the "good old days." Grandmom was just about the best cook in the entire universe, and if you announced she was coming for dinner, it was certain you would have a house full of happy people with great appetites. If all the aunts were together, it would only take one to start, and there would be a sing-along, with everyone joining in. The little ones would usually giggle when the singing began then bob their heads to the tunes or watch with awe. These gatherings most likely will be cherished moments long remembered.

After the company left and Mom and I finished the dishes, we went to a parish mission and motivational lecture. Upon our return home, Billy told us he was experiencing severe pain in his joints. My heart sank, as we had had such a good day, only to be clouded by another call to the hospital. Not certain if this was a normal reaction after this particular round of chemotherapy, the on-call doctor suggested Billy take Motrin to decrease the joint inflammation, but as a precaution, he wanted Billy seen by Dr. Michaels the following morning for a complete work up. Billy's immune system was compromised due to the chemotherapy, and it was vital to test for infection at the first symptom. Naturally, Billy was disappointed knowing he had to go back to Jefferson, but I assured him the visit was solely for the purpose of precautionary testing and the doctor had no intention of admitting him. Luckily, as the night progressed, the Motrin proved to be effective, and Billy was able to get a good night's sleep. Matthew and Sean slept downstairs with Billy so he wouldn't be alone during the night if he began to feel ill. They were so protective of their big brother and wanted to spend every chance they could with him.

Billy's dad agreed to take him to see Dr. Michaels, allowing me to work in the New Jersey office for a few hours. I planned to meet them for lunch and make a decision based on his test results, either return to the office or stay home with Billy. As it turned out, Billy's port was blocked, preventing the doctors from getting a blood return. Billy had to have the port re-accessed, which resulted in him spending most of the day at the hospital. Once Billy finally returned home, he was exhausted and a little hungry. While I prepared dinner, he recounted the events of the day. After we enjoyed a nice family dinner, Kevin and his girl-friend, Korrin, visited with Billy in the evening. That made his day. He was so glad to be home and have visitors. The next few days were even better for Billy. He was finally sleeping at night and eating three meals daily. His appetite was actually improv-ing. One day he was tantalized by a Red Lobster commercial and couldn't wait to go out to eat. I was getting paid on Friday, so I promised him a Red Lobster dinner, and we went as a family. It was great to go out to eat together. We enjoyed each other's company in a neutral setting, and we were able to relax and talk and laugh without the hospital bed or even the medicine drawers at home staring us in the face. Moments like that we cherish and remember, plain and simple.

Billy worked passionately on his cousin Anthony's Pinewood Derby car over the next few days, being precise in its weight and size measurements. Once the car met the exact specifications and Billy was satisfied with his work, he contacted Anthony for a final okay. Anthony visited Billy over the weekend and they painted the car together. Once the paint had dried, he brought his car home. Anthony was so happy and grateful Billy had helped him with his car. He loved it, and Billy was honored Anthony asked him to help.

The following weekend we had a lot of visitors. Bob and Dawn came with the kids from Connecticut, and my brother Bill and his boys came from Greenville, Pennsylvania. His youngest son, also named William, suddenly came down with a cold or a stomach virus and had to stay at my mother's house. With my Billy's immune system so compromised, we had to screen our visitors. I always had hand sanitizer by the front door as you entered, masks and rubber gloves on days his counts were low. Being obsessive compulsive, I cleaned my house with bleach to kill any germs. I was terribly fearful of Billy contracting any type of infection, and although I felt bad, I couldn't risk having anyone with any type of sniffle or germ enter the house. I knew my nephew wanted to see Billy so badly, but it was a sacrifice he had to make for his cousin.

I made a large turkey dinner, and my sister-in-law Dawn brought a large pan of lasagna. My nephew Vinny and niece Abby kept me company in the afternoon while we made desserts and my sister, JoAnne, and her boys walked in with an additional assortment of cakes and pies. It was like Thanksgiving dinner in February. Billy was so happy to have a houseful of company. He was even more excited to be able to sit with us at the table and actually have an appetite and enjoy the feast. Even more so, Billy was happy because it had been so long since all of his cousins had been together around the table, and he was happy to be a part of it. At that time, two of my brothers lived quite a distance away, and with the inclement weather during the winter, it was too dangerous to travel during the holiday season, but this weekend they all made it safely. Their sacrifices meant so much to Billy, whether they realized it or not.

After the company left on Sunday, things were pretty quiet at the house. I was afraid Billy might get depressed since everyone left, but, rather, Billy was feeling so well that he was full of energy and couldn't sit still. He gave his boss, Bob, a call and told him he would be able to go with him on Monday to look at new trucks for the stone yard. He was so excited to still be involved with the stone yard and be around all the equipment and trucks. Only the little things in life made him so happy.

Billy continued to keep himself busy the next few days. He even stopped by the girls' basketball game at his alma mater elementary school and talked to many old friends who had also dropped in. Everyone repeatedly told him how good he looked. They were so glad to have run into him, and they wished him continued progress with his treatments and promised to keep their prayers going.

At Billy's next appointment with Dr. Michaels, on February 26, 1998, both she and Rocco were amazed at his progress. They told him he had reached another milestone, that he had progressed spectacularly with his weight and he could finally stop the TPN at night. Billy was thrilled when he heard that. It wasn't that running the TPN pump at night was a problem; it was just an inconvenience whenever he made plans to go out, as he would be a slave to the clock and make sure he could get home in time to start the pump for the twelve hours. Just the fact that they were taking the line out made him happy. The next day, Ryan came to the house and removed the port, and we made him take all the TPN we had left in the refrigerator. Billy took advantage of his freedom from the pump and went out with Kevin, not getting home until after midnight. He said it was great not having to rush home for the TPN. He felt like a regular teenager, if only for a few brief days.

Billy had been shopping for dirt bikes with his friend Matt, a truck driver at the stone yard. Billy and Matt became fast friends. Matt was a big influence on Billy, as he too was a bike rider and they would ride together. When Billy found the bike he wanted, it was hard to tell him how fearful I was to see him riding a dirt bike. I knew he had to take every precaution not to injure himself, and he too knew his limitations. But on the other hand, he was a nineteen-year-old teenager who wanted to enjoy life and have fun. How could you tell your child who had suffered so much that he couldn't have fun? I expressed my fears, but I did, nonetheless, share his enthusiasm for adventure, and I wanted him to be happy. Matt went with Billy to look at the dirt bike and agreed that it was a good deal. He also offered to get the bike home for Billy on the back of his Mustang with the trailer hitch. Billy was excited, and it was great to see him so happy. It was only a brief few days of fun, however, as we were scheduled to begin round five in a couple of days.

Round Five

March 2, 1998, Billy's dad took Billy to the hospital to get started with round five so I could get a few things done at the office. Billy had to be in by ten thirty in the morning, but again, they didn't start the chemo until the next day. I continued to call Billy from the office every hour or so, and when I spoke to him after lunch, he told me they had just started the IV fluids at one thirty in the afternoon. I called again about an hour later, and he was livid. They still had not started the chemotherapy, and he was deeply distressed about it. Every extra hour in the hospital was one too many for Billy. He wanted to do so much in a day, and sitting around the hospital for someone to administer liquids or medications was just a bit too irritating for him. I could understand his anxiety and displeasure in the lack of communication regarding his therapy sessions, so I called down to Dr. Michaels's office and spoke with her physician's assistant, Diane, who explained to me that it was a prerequisite for Billy to be fully hydrated for at least twelve hours prior to beginning this round of chemotherapy. Why this was never explained to us in advance will remain a mystery. Diane further said there was difficulty getting a blood return on Billy's port. They had accessed it, and fluids went in, but they couldn't get a blood return from it. As a result, the nurses had to do the labs through the veins in Billy's arms. His platelet count was a little low at nine, and they wanted it a bit higher. Then they had to check his stool for blood.

Dr. Flander visited Billy's room a few times that afternoon and advised Billy that the delay was partially due to the port being blocked and said she would check with Dr. Michaels and get back to Billy as to when they could possibly start the chemotherapy. Rocco subsequently entered into Billy's room before I left work, and when Billy complained to him, his response was simply "The orders were written. I did my part."

Billy was not happy with that response, and he immediately called me at the office. By then I had just about finished the assignment I was working on and told him was going to get the boys some dinner and head on up to the hospital. I stopped at McDonald's for them then ran to the Mall. I needed a few small items, and I wanted to get more pajama pants for Billy. After a few quick purchases, we headed for the car, when I realized I did not have my car keys. The boys and I frantically retraced our steps through the department store and came up empty. The store manager assisted us in looking, and, sure enough, there they were at the bottom of the wallet display, covered by several layers of leather. I thanked the manager and the boys and I literally ran out of the store. What was to be a simple, quick errand turned out to be a distressing hour-long project stressing on all of our nerves.

By the time the boys and I got to the hospital, we were finally able to laugh about the incident when we relayed it to Billy. He just looked at me in amazement and chuckled. "Only you, Mom. Only you." He said it was fine that we were a few minutes late, as they still didn't start the chemotherapy, and there was no way they were going to start it that night. I did, however, get to

Billy's room before Dr. Michaels had a chance to stop in. She arrived with Dr. Flander, and they tried to explain to Billy why the delay in chemotherapy was due, in part, to the blocked port. I explained how distressed Billy was and also advised her of how unprepared the room was. Not only was the staff unprepared to administer chemotherapy, but the room had never been cleaned prior to Billy's admittance. I questioned Dr. Michaels as to the importance of a clean, disinfected room and wondered why and how this could have happened on a floor that administers chemotherapy to patients on a continuous basis. I believe I was a bit more upset over the lack of cleanliness in the room than Billy was, but nevertheless, it was an issue that needed to be addressed. So off to the director of nursing administrator we went.

The room was cleaned and disinfected while Billy, his brothers, and I took a walk to the other side of the hospital to the snack machine. We sat in the lounge for a little while and stopped to talk with one of the nurses who took a special interest in Billy. On our way back to his room, we ran into another male nurse Billy had befriended, Karl, who asked us why we were on the other side of the hospital. We explained our little escape from the room, exchanged good wishes, and then proceeded back to our room. When we returned to the room, we found it cleaned and refreshed. The scent of clean linen sheets permeated the air, and there was a surprise sitting on Billy's desk, a VCR. Billy was thrilled someone had finally remembered, and immediately he selected a movie. We put *Independence Day* in the VCR, and it hadn't even played for half an hour before Billy was fast asleep. It was good to see him finally sleep so soundly. I loved to see him looking so peaceful and sleeping pain free, so I decided to wash up for the evening and curl up on the leather chair by his bed while the boys tried to get comfortable on the leather window seat.

We were up by five thirty the next morning for blood work and vitals. Breakfast was served at eight o'clock, and I called the office and took the day off. I knew they would most likely be starting the chemotherapy sometime that day, and there was no way I was going to leave Billy alone all day again. I was going to be there just in case there was any change in the plans and the chemo didn't get started. I wasn't going to allow him to get upset unnecessarily a second time. The morning nurse on duty was kind enough to bring us some literature on the VP-16 and ifosfamide, two of the drugs being used in that segment of the protocol. The information she gave us appeared to be quite similar to the printout we received from the pharmacy. We read the printed material and just sat in Billy's room most of the morning with the boys. Billy requested a back rub, and then after a short nap, we watched another movie. Just before lunch, the dietician went in to see Billy. She asked him if there was anything special he wanted to see on his trays and if there were any special snacks he would be interested in between meals and in the evening. They wanted him to increase his caloric intake, and if there was anything he wanted, she said to just let her know and she would make sure he had it. Billy requested ham and cheese sandwiches to come in the afternoon and evening, and she promised to fulfill his desire. She also suggested that he have a milkshake in the afternoon, and he agreed.

Dr. Michaels and Dr. Flander went back in to see Billy at two thirty in the afternoon and told Billy how well he was taking all of this. They emphasized that he was getting extremely large doses of chemo and he had tolerated it well. Dr. Flander increased Billy's fluids and reduced the amount of sodium in his IV. His urine was somewhat concentrated, and he should have been drinking a little more water during the day. They were watching for edema, especially in the legs, and they had Billy getting up and about as much as possible while in the hospital.

One night Rocco went into Billy's room and discussed the advantages of going to the bone marrow transplant unit early, possibly for his next round of chemo. He suggested Billy get familiar with the unit and the staff before he actually had to be admitted. He proposed Billy have chemotherapy treatments six and seven there. The bone marrow unit agreed to have Billy admitted prior to his transplant; Rocco had made the arrangements prior to addressing them to Billy, but we did not know that at the time. He summarized all the activities they had available—the Internet, stationery bike, treadmill, and other gym equipment on request from rehab. Billy and I exchanged glances and agreed it sounded like a good idea, but we would see what happened when the time came; I didn't want to set Billy up for another disappointment. We met Dr. Folley and his staff, and Billy was excited to be on that unit; it was I who was hesitant. Billy couldn't take another letdown, not after all he had been through. I wasn't going to let that happen if I could at all prevent it.

The next few days were typical for Billy in the hospital, up by seven in the morning, the nurses would take his vitals, then breakfast would come. If Billy was feeling up to it, I would start a movie before heading to the office for a few hours. If Billy was having a bad day or if I felt he needed a little more attention, I would skip the office in the morning and play it by ear after lunch. If Billy's back was bothering him, I would offer to give him a back rub, and he would just relax in my arms. It was comforting for me to be able to give my son a few minutes of relief. If I was able to decrease his pain in any way, I was more than happy to do it. It was my one and only wish to make all his pain disappear and have my son whole again and live an active lifestyle. There were moments we both wished for days gone by, and then we realized we couldn't go back. We must move forward. There wasn't much we could do in this situation but hope and pray for the best, and you can be sure we did our share of praying. I prayed with every waking breath for my son to be healed. Family and friends were praying. There were prayer chains around the world being said for my son, a lot of prayers.

Billy's discharge from this round of chemotherapy was delayed due to a urinary tract infection. Billy was prepared to be in the hospital for five days of chemotherapy and then home as quickly as he could. He was a bit disappointed when, every subsequent day, his labs came back with either an infection or a fever. Matt and Sean took turns sleeping at the hospital with me. Matt enjoyed staying at the hospital, and oftentimes he said he would like to stay during the week and possibly miss a day or two of school. I chuckled at his suggestion and reminded him that he was just getting back on track with his studies and there was no way I was going to let him miss any school.

By the sixth night in the hospital, Billy began to get a little depressed. We would sit on the window seat outside of his room and chat about the cancer, his wonderful attitude, the recovery process, and life in general. Billy said he felt he had suffered a lot during his life. He was thinking about a traumatic incident that had occurred back in 1993—then about how he almost lost a finger from the electric trimmer while doing a lawn job—and now this. He recalled the bad luck with his car when he was in the parking lot at the local convenience store and backed into another. Although there was no damage at all, the owner of the car was a very rude and obnoxious woman who wanted the insurance company to pay for damages that did not exist. It turned out to be a major pain in the neck. Nevertheless, Billy was honest about the scratch and stayed in the parking lot until the woman returned to her car, and he gave her all of his insurance information. He was an honest young man, and he was fair and truthful. That was the way he was brought up, and he believed others would react the same way. It was a hard lesson to learn. The world is full of all different kinds of people, and not all of them are honest or fair, and it was discouraging for Billy to learn firsthand.

Billy acknowledged how hard he always had to work for things he wanted, yet he enjoyed working hard and earning an honest day's living. I interjected and reminded Billy of all the good times he had experienced and said to focus on that. I told him he must thank God for all of his blessings and for all that he did have. He had a family who loved him very much, we had a nice house, he had two nice cars, a truck, two motorcycles, and so on. He acknowledged all the good, but he repeated that he always worked hard to get the things that he wanted. We spoke a little about material things and how they were immaterial. I reminded him of all the saints that suffered and how our Lord suffered and died for all of us. I didn't have the answers he wanted to hear, and I don't know that I will ever have the answer. We both shed a few tears. I gave him a back rub, and then we went for a walk.

On the day of his discharge, we were waiting for the on-call doctor to sign the discharge papers. When he finally appeared sometime in the afternoon, he said he was waiting on Billy's hemoglobin counts and his urine specimen. The hemoglobin from the port came back at five, so the doctor had the nurse draw the blood peripherally, and she sent it to the lab stat, and it came back at the count of ten. When the urine specimen came back within normal limits, we knew the discharge papers would be signed. We finally left the hospital at nine o'clock in the evening.

Billy was thrilled to be home. Matthew and Sean were out playing street hockey, so Billy went into the house and asked me to start the TPN so he could climb into bed and get a good night's sleep. The next few nights were uneventful. Billy was able to sleep comfortably in his own bed, a waterbed, I might add, with a heater. He was cozy under the covers and had lots of company around him. Matthew and Sean slept in his room with him, sometimes even on the waterbed, but most of the time in a sleeping bag on the floor next to him. On the days when Billy just wasn't feeling too well, he would sleep either on the sofa or on the leather recliner in the family room downstairs, just next to Billy's room. It was a rare night that Billy would have to sleep alone. If neither of the boys were home, I would always sleep downstairs and keep him company.

By his third night home, Billy began to experience pain in his joints. Ryan continued to come to the house and draw Billy's labs. He said between the rainy weather and the type of chemotherapy Billy was on, joint pain was not unusual. Although Billy was getting up almost every two hours to go to the bathroom, he was still able to get a good night's sleep. He was revitalized most of the days, and he enjoyed taking the boys to the batting cages or to a movie. If they did not go to the movie theater, they would rent a movie of their choice and watch it on the VCR. All three of my boys were real movie buffs, and it was always so heartwarming for me to see them enjoy the films together. I can only imagine how they relive those precious moments today, watching a movie they sat through with their brother. I know myself that when I see a movie Billy and I watched together, it tugs at my heartstrings, and I can't help but get teary eyed.

Now that Billy was back on the TPN pump, there were nights when it did not always cooperate with us. Sometimes Billy would wake up to find the TPN pump had never even dispensed the liquid protein nutrition. We just couldn't figure out what was going on with that darn pump, so we had the nurse come to the house to see if there was a malfunction in the pump or if it was I. (It was the pump.) When Ryan came to the house a few days later, he was unable to get a blood return from the port again. We called Dr. Michaels's office, and she advised us to get to her office immediately the next morning. I was not to run the TPN, nor was I to flush the line until she saw it in the morning. When we arrived at her office, it was determined that the port would have to be removed. It appeared to be resting on the vein and rubbing, causing inflammation. Since the port was necessary for the next round of chemotherapy, we had to make arrangements as quickly as possible to have it replaced. The removal of the port and the implantation of another line had to be performed surgically. Billy was not thrilled to be heading to the operating room again, and he voiced his displeasure to the doctors.

All I could think of was how much this poor kid had been through. He wondered how much more he could endure. I just prayed repeatedly, hoping for the end of this ordeal for him. I just wanted him to finish his treatments and get back to a normal teenage life. I realized, however, that with all he had been through, there was no way his life would ever be the same. He would never be able to return to a normal teenage lifestyle. He had matured and been through too much. He would, however, be able to return to a somewhat active lifestyle and enjoy his cars, trucks, and motorcycles and, most specially, fishing with his friends. He was truly my special angel and a very special child. God bless my Billy!

It had been a bitter cold winter, but while he was home, Billy continued to keep himself busy at the stone yard. He would go to the Palmyra yard some days with his friend Matt, and they would work on trucks or some other equipment. Billy was happy when he was in his element, and big diesel trucks were certainly his element. Some days he would leave around six forty-five in the morning and not get home until almost two o'clock in the afternoon. He would come home from work exhausted, but he wouldn't succumb to the weakness, not just yet. He would take a nap in the afternoon and be ready for activity with either his brothers or Kevin in the evening. I was happy to see him up and about, living as normal a life as possible, and, more than that, he was eating!

A few times, he would express a desire to go to Nicole's apartment, but I continuously reminded him of the cats she had. On one particular evening, he and I actually went back and forth, arguing about the dangers of being around cats. I was a nervous wreck. If the doctor said to stay away from cats, I wanted him to stay away from cats. Billy's reasoning to me was that if he could go to Nan's house, and she had a cat, then why couldn't he go to his sister's house? I explained to him that his counts were low and his chance of infection was greatest at this time. But I left the final decision in his hands. I was not going to tell him he could not visit his sister, but I did suggest Nicole come home to visit with him. Maybe I went a little too far with the precautions and consequences of him getting an infection. He said he would not go now but would remember this discussion the next time we go to Nan's. I couldn't continue the conversation of how clean Nan's house was and how differently Nicole and her roommates kept their apartment. Rather, I just put it in his hands and said, "It's your decision, Billy. I won't tell you what to do, but I will always love you and look out for your best interests."

Later that evening, Billy took Sean to Blockbuster and rented a movie to watch. I started the TPN, and we all fell asleep. I was torn when I looked at my son sleeping. He was beautiful, his heart was as big as the world, and he would give you the shirt off his back. Now, looking at him exhausted, thin, and pale, I could only say a prayer and ask that God continue to watch over him and help him persevere through this ordeal. I knew we had a long road ahead of us, but we would travel it together.

The day before Nicole's birthday, Billy awakened feeling sick. He had a temperature of 101.3 degrees, and his body was sore and aching. He just wanted to stay in bed and sleep, but his ultrasound was scheduled for later that morning. Bill brought Billy to Jefferson for his appointment, and I spent most of the morning fighting with the insurance company for approval for the procedure. The insurance company was willing to pay for the test at the local radiology center close to home, but they did not understand why we had to have the test performed at the hospital. Thankfully, we finally did get approval for the test but a warning that any and all future ultrasound studies must be done at the radiology center they selected.

Billy's fever continued throughout the following day, and since we had another appointment at Jefferson, we called Dr. Michaels's office and advised her of Billy's fever. She told us to go to her office after our consult with Dr. Berber. Billy and I met with Dr. Berber around nine thirty in the morning, and she was thorough. She discovered a small blood clot behind the port and felt a few days of Coumadin would eliminate it. She also said Billy would need to have a PICC line inserted prior to the next round of chemotherapy; an appointment was made.

With all of this talk about inserting a new line and blood clots, I was extremely nervous. Anxiety set in, and I wanted to talk to Dr. Michaels and have all of this explained to me slowly. It seemed they were playing with medications and testing the waters. I didn't want anyone administering anything to Billy without the advice of Dr. Kushner at Sloan-Kettering or someone from Dr. Michaels's office. I called Dr. Michaels's office and left a detailed message on her voice mail. When she finally called home, it was after five o'clock in the evening, and Billy answered the phone. Dr. Michaels told him they might not have to remove the old port now. She would consult with Dr. Berber and get back to us. Billy was relieved that there was a chance he didn't have to go through another procedure with CVIR, but on the other hand, he was concerned about whether the old port would continue to be a nuisance. She did not mention anything to him regarding the Coumadin for the blood clots. Shortly after Billy spoke with Dr. Michaels, Ryan called and said he would voice mail Diane in Dr. Michaels's office and have someone get back to us. He said that he was equally confused now too about the ports and that he would be at our house in the morning between nine and ten o'clock.

We had a houseful for dinner, as it was Nicole's twenty-first birthday. We had our traditional ham and cabbage and corned beef and potatoes for dinner, as it was March 17. Later, those over twenty-one went to Houlihan's for Nicole to have a legal drink. Then everyone went home. Billy and the boys watched a movie while I washed the dishes, vacuumed, laundered the table-cloths, and later relaxed in the tub. Another day. Another long, full day, but another fond memory.

Ryan was at our house by nine thirty in the morning the following day as promised. He drew Billy's labs then contacted Dr.
Mike's office for the necessary referrals, as he was our primary
physician. Dr. Mike requested to speak directly to Dr. Michaels
for specific information regarding the referral. I left several messages for Dr. Michaels with Dr. Mike's telephone number and
instructed her to call him as soon as possible if she needed the
referral. When I finally heard from Dr. Michaels, she explained
that we needed a referral for CVIR and one for her office visit.
I was totally confused then because she was requesting a referral for a new port. She had just told Billy two days prior that he
might not need the port, and now she was talking a new port
again. She said we would discuss all of this the following day
in her office. Later that evening we received a call from a doctor at Jefferson in the radiology department advising that Billy
should fast from midnight "in case they had to sedate him for the
PICC line."

I was confused at the mention of a PICC line. "What PICC
line? For what?" This was the first I had heard of that, and I
explained to the doctor there was to be no surgical intervention
until after we cleared it with Dr. Michaels. I was confused, and
Billy was confused and anxious. Then he began to feel nauseous.
He was tired, and his back hurt. I administered his injections
and rubbed his back. He wasn't sure if he felt hungry or not then
decided to just get into bed early and try to sleep it off. I told him
I had everything documented in the notebook and we would read
it all back to Dr. Michaels and clear it up at our appointment. It
would be taken care of, and it wasn't anything for him to worry
about. Doctors consult and change their minds all the time.

Billy was seen by the doctor in CVIR the following morning
who was very informative. He seemed to explain things to Billy
and answered all of his questions regarding the PICC line and
the port. Billy liked the way he described the procedures to him.
He told Billy the clot was probably very small and could move

slightly. The doctor said Billy shouldn't experience any symptoms with it, and he felt the port should come out eventually. If we could get fluid in, they should leave it for the next two chemotherapies and then remove it and have a whole new port inserted for the bone marrow transplant. This doctor also suggested we not bother with the PICC line, as it was an inconvenience, and it would only be for two chemos, and why undergo additional procedures? He said it should be Billy's decision because it would mean that he could only use the port for chemo. In other words, he would have to be stuck for all his labs. It would be up to him. If he didn't mind getting stuck for a few more weeks, we should leave the port alone.

Billy said he was going to get stuck any way and he didn't think the PICC line would make a difference. Clearly, he didn't like the idea of the PICC line procedure. He didn't mind keeping this port as long as there were no health risks and/or future problems caused by the blood clot. Billy asked if it posed a problem with the port pressing on the vein wall. The doctor explained that it was not the ideal situation, and it could cause infection and discomfort, but they used soft catheters and it should be okay for a short period of time. The doctor went on to further question Billy about his kidney function and whether or not he was experiencing back pain. Billy acknowledged that his back had been bothering him the past few nights but said it was not a constant issue. The doctor said there was a risk of stents getting blocked and that could cause the kidneys to become enlarged and malfunction. Billy said he hoped the stents were not blocked, of course, and so did I. That doctor spent a lot of time with us, and he was very informative and down to earth, explaining all possibilities to us.

From CVIR we waited in Dr. Michaels's office for her nursing assistant to draw Billy's labs. The nurse informed us at that time that Dr. Michaels never told her to make arrangements for Billy's chemo the following week. Thus, the insurance company had not been called for precertification, nor was a hospital room reserved for him. I then asked Dr. Michaels if she was still contemplating moving Billy's surgery ahead of the last chemotherapy or not. She said she wasn't sure and asked me to "please not hold her" to anything. She wasn't prepared to address that issue at this time, and she would get back to us on that. I asked why it was even mentioned if she wasn't prepared to address it. She went on to explain that Billy's case was a little different than the usual P6 protocol. "Typically the surgery is performed after the third round of chemotherapy, but Billy's tumor was so large and involved, we had to operate first," she said. She promised to do more research and consult with Dr. Kushner and then get back to us. She then informed us that we were going to move forward with round six of the chemotherapy the following Monday, as Billy's counts were up to 32,000. There was some concern regarding his hemoglobin counts, however; they were a little low. She wanted me to continue with the Epogen injections, and his counts would be checked again prior to Monday.

The following few days, Billy had little energy. The days were dark and dreary, as we had a rainy period. He did continue to go to the yard, but his stamina was low, and he only stayed about an hour each day. We occupied most of our time working on a baseball puzzle and watching television in his room. We were thrilled when Sean placed the last puzzle piece on the board. It was a family production, providing each of us downtime and a sense of accomplishment when finally complete.

On Sunday night prior to Billy starting round six of chemotherapy, Billy treated Kevin to the Flyers game. Phyllis's dad gave them the tickets, including the parking, so Billy only thought it fair to invite Chad, Phyllis's son and Matthew's good friend, to join him and Kevin. They didn't get home until after midnight, but they had a great time at the game. Billy was tired and anxious about the next round of chemotherapy. He knew each round brought us closer to the completion of P6, and he nervously awaited the end result. We all did.

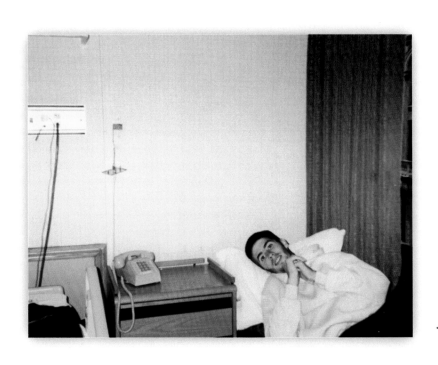

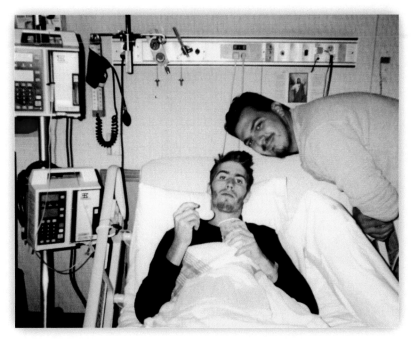

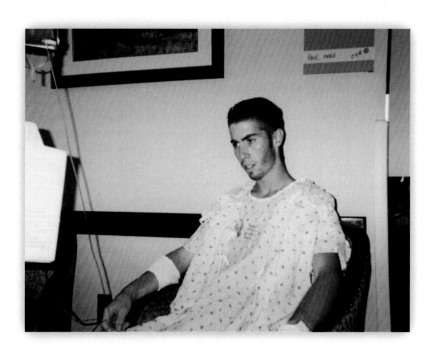

Round Six

Billy's dad took him to the hospital on the morning scheduled for the next round of chemotherapy. While we usually waited hours before the start of the actual infusion, I decided to take advantage of the time I could spend at the office before treatment started. When I called Billy in the early afternoon to see how he was feeling, I learned they hadn't yet started the IV fluids. Furious, I called Dr. Michaels's office and questioned the delayed start and asked why the orders weren't even signed for his chemotherapy. As a result of my phone call, Dr. Michaels called down to Billy's room and spoke with him herself and explained that his specific gravity, which is a laboratory test that measures the concentration of all chemical particles in the urine, was 10.0, and they wanted the numbers to be around a 10.12 or a 12.10; he couldn't remember exactly what she said. Knowing the chemotherapy would not be starting for quite some time, I asked Billy if it would be okay for me to take advantage of the time and put in a full day of work. He was completely in agreement with my decision and said he would look for me after

153

work. After work, I decided to take the boys to McDonald's for dinner, and then we all went to the hospital. We brought cheeseburgers for both Bill and Billy. They were both grateful for the treat. Afterward, Matthew and I took a stroll down to the cafeteria for some coffee, and we went back to the room and waited and waited and waited for the chemotherapy to begin.

Around nine o'clock that evening, Billy brought to our attention a lump on the top of his port. As soon as I mentioned it to the nurse, she made a call to the doctor. In the meantime, while she was trying to get a blood return, the port wouldn't work. She tried both sides, and still no blood return. Her next step was to put a separate IV line in for the fluids, and then she ran a blood return and waited for the labs to come back before she started the chemotherapy. In the meantime, Dr. Soto looked at the port, and he wasn't comfortable using the port for the chemotherapy. He said the chemo was extremely toxic, and if the port were to leak, it could burn Billy's skin. He recommended a PICC line or another type of line for temporary use. He said it was Billy's choice. He could have had another line inserted at that time and start chemotherapy, or he could have chosen to wait and see Dr. Michaels the following day.

While the nurse was explaining the procedure to Billy, a doctor from interventional radiology explained the specifics of the surgical procedure for a PICC line. He told Billy the line would go into a vein in his chest but only for this chemotherapy. He informed us of the possible side effects and dangers of the procedure, including puncture of the lungs. This was not something I wanted Billy to go through, but he did not want to wait another day before starting the chemotherapy, so he signed the consent form for the procedure. About an hour later, after they checked the blood clot factors, a third doctor came in to explain the procedure more thoroughly to Billy, again stating that the line would go into his vein in his chest and they would most likely begin the procedure shortly.

After waiting another hour or two, a team of doctors entered Billy's hospital room and advised that they wanted to put a PICC line in Billy's groin rather than in his chest because there was less chance of infection. Neither Billy nor I was comfortable with this. We asked why this was never mentioned by any of the three doctors that were in earlier. We were told it was much safer and it was for Billy's protection to have the line in the femoral vein in the groin. Billy asked if this meant they had to go into his groin area every time they changed or refilled the chemotherapy and fluid lines. The doctor responded negatively and said they would have extensions on the lines. Billy hesitantly gave his consent, but only because he did not want to wait another day for the chemotherapy regimen. I tried to persuade him to wait until the morning and discuss this with Dr. Michaels, but he was adamant about going home on Thursday. There was no way he wanted to spend an extra day in the hospital. He felt he lost all day waiting for the doctors to make up their minds about administering the chemotherapy, and he had made plans for the weekend. He wanted to go home, and that was the bottom line.

The procedure took about forty-five minutes, and it was performed right there in Billy's room while the boys and I waited nervously outside in the hall. When the doctor told me the procedure went well, he said Billy had to lie still until the nurse applied the dressing over the sutures, but I was permitted to go into his room. We waited over half an hour before we saw a nurse go in to apply the dressing. I had to ask her to please dress the wound because Billy had to go to the bathroom. It was then that the nurse informed us that Billy wasn't getting his chemotherapy started that evening because his urine had blood in it.

I thought Billy was going to blow a gasket. Astonished, I questioned the nurse as to when this blood was drawn, as this was the first time there was any mention of blood in his urine. There were routine blood tests done all day. This was the first time we had heard anything about blood in his urine. I too was angry at that point, and asked to speak to the doctor. We had been communicating with the doctor most of the day, and were informed that as soon as the line was in, they were prepared to start the chemotherapy. I had conversations and blood test results documented. What was she talking about? Had there been mention of blood in his urine and a delay in the chemotherapy, there was no way Billy would have consented to having a femoral line inserted in his groin. He certainly would not have chosen to have a surgical procedure knowing that he would have to wait an extra day before they even began his treatment. Neither of us could comprehend what they were doing. It seemed as if one doctor was looking at one set of records and the nursing staff was looking at another. I immediately placed another call to Dr. Michaels. This time I wanted her paged. I demanded to speak to her directly and not anyone else.

It was getting late in the evening, and the chemotherapy still was not started. Dr. Michaels still had not returned my page, and Billy was getting more and more unsettled. I asked the nurse for a copy of the lab reports that showed blood in his urine and was told they were not available. Frustrated, I decided to take a walk to the west wing of the hospital, searching for a familiar face. When I came upon a nurse who had cared for Billy on a previous hospital stay, we greeted each other with a hug and exchanged niceties. She asked what I was doing on the west wing, and I explained the trouble we were experiencing during this round of chemotherapy and was bold enough to ask if there were any rooms available on the west side. Since we knew most of the nurses on that wing, they were sympathetic to our request and gave me the number to the nursing supervisor, hoping she could assist us.

In the meantime, the doctor who inserted the femoral line wandered down the hall, and I stopped him. I asked him the reason why he was not willing to start the chemotherapy after he subjected my son to the pain and inconvenience of a femoral line in his groin. He responded that the nurse advised him that Billy's labs showed evidence of blood since the afternoon. This was news to me, as we were never advised of blood in his urine at all, especially since we were questioning the delay in the chemotherapy and the issues with Billy's port. We were consistently told the reason for the delay in starting his chemotherapy was due to the blocked port. Never, not once, did anyone mention blood in his urine. I then proceeded to tell the doctors that Billy had stents and there was always a trace of blood in his urine due to the stents. I asked him if he or the nurse advising him were aware of the stents and if they had even looked further into his labs to know that. He seemed to be clueless as to the stents and simply responded with, "I am not comfortable giving chemotherapy with his urine numbers, and I have the authority to hold the chemotherapy."

Back in Billy's room, with tears in my eyes, I told him how sorry I was that he had undergone such a painful procedure and for naught. I had to tell him the doctor refused to administer the chemotherapy due to the blood in his urine and we would most likely have to wait until Dr. Michaels returned our call. Neither of us could figure out why the doctor even bothered with the femoral line if he had no intention of starting the therapy. We were both angry, and I intended to report this incident.

The nursing supervisor went down to Billy's room. After I went through the events of the day and what appeared to be a runaround between the nurses and the doctors regarding Billy's chemotherapy and labs and the femoral line procedure, she said she would look into the matter. Within an hour, the doctor who refused to administer the chemotherapy suddenly entered Billy's room and announced they were going to start the chemo. When I asked what changed, he admitted to reviewing Billy's chart personally and said that he was misinformed by the nurses regarding his previous urine specimens and that it was okay to start the chemotherapy. I was flabbergasted. I asked him if I had heard him correctly in that he never looked at Billy's chart before making a decision to start the chemotherapy or not. He simply relied on the nurses' verbal relay of information. I questioned whether it was standard procedure to subject a patient to a painful femoral line procedure based on what a nurse told him and asked, "Shouldn't a licensed physician read a patient's chart before any type of invasive surgical procedure?"

Billy and I pointed out to him that we had informed him of the stents and that because of them there was always a trace amount of blood in his urine. I even asked for a copy of his labs to compare them to the previous labs, and, of course, I was denied this request. I told him I was always given a copy of Billy's labs, and it was never an issue. Why was I denied a copy this time? If he was willing to listen to what the nurses had to say, why wasn't he willing to listen to what we were trying to tell him? As it turns out, we were correct. It was the stents that caused the trace amounts of blood in his urine, and had he only taken the time to read his chart or compare his labs, we could have avoided this entire incident. I made him a bit uneasy. Actually, I made this doctor downright angry. He responded in a sarcastic tone that if I thought there was something I said or did to intimidate him into starting the chemotherapy, I was mistaken. Billy and I knew we hit a nerve, so we simply ended the conversation there. He was initiating the chemotherapy, regardless. It was now three o'clock in the morning, but Billy was happy to get it started, and the delay only held back his discharge a few hours. That was the bottom line for Billy, so we left it at that.

For the most part, we had the best of care with the nurses and the physicians during our hospital stay. This particular wing of the third floor was an unfortunate experience for us, and we made sure we never stayed there again. The nursing supervisor assured us of handling the situation, and Dr. Michaels was made aware of the ordeal. Naturally, she was annoyed that Billy had undergone the femoral line procedure, and as soon as she returned to the hospital, it was removed. We learned a lesson from this unpleasant experience and never allowed anyone to suggest or perform anything invasive or questionable again.

Before Billy was discharged after he completed this round of chemotherapy, he was scheduled to have a heart-function test. He was hooked up to an EKG machine, and a nuclear camera recorded the heart activity. The name of the test was called a multigated acquisition. I was told this was a standard test performed after one received such high-volume chemotherapy. He was also scheduled for a pulmonary function test as an outpatient. They knew Billy was weak and nauseous from the chemotherapy and felt he would perform better after he regained some of his strength and endurance.

The day after Billy was discharged, he experienced weakness and joint pain. He went to the stone yard for about an hour but had to return home to take a nap. He went to the store with his dad to pick up a new screen door for the patio but didn't have the strength to help install it. He said his dad ran into some difficulties installing the door, and it appeared to be comic. He said that he wished he had a camera and that it should have been taped for *America's Funniest Home Videos*. We all laughed when he retold the story to us, as we know his dad isn't very mechanically inclined and is hand-tool challenged.

The laughter soon brought tears to our eyes. Billy began to apologize for not being able to help his dad install the patio door. He was angry that he didn't have the stamina he once had and apologized for not being able to help with things around the house like he used to. He got depressed and said he wasn't sure how much more he could take. He said he had had enough. Hearing him apologize and seeing how depressed he was, I began to cry. It wasn't too long thereafter that we both were crying.

I reminded Billy of all he had accomplished, all he had overcome, and how proud I was of his strength. He had been so courageous, and it was his determination and zeal for life that boosted his progress. I commented on how noble he was and that he couldn't quit now. I asked him to be strong for both he and for me. He said he didn't want to see me cry; I said I would try to be strong for him and try to hold back the tears. I explained how this was wearing both of us down and that we needed our strength now more than ever. We'd been through the worst, and now we must persevere through the rest. I prayed fervently that night to God to give us both the strength to carry this cross. Father Sylvestor, called me that very evening. He is such a spiritual man, always knew when we needed a friend. He said Billy and I were again on his mind and that he and the other friars were keeping us in their daily prayers, and he asked that we continue to keep him posted on Billy's progress. I believe with all my heart that it was the urging of our guardian angels for him to make that call to me, as we truly needed to hear an encouraging word of faith and hope that particular night.

Trial Run

On April 2, 1998, Billy had an appointment with Dr. Michaels. He was complaining of a sore throat and had not slept much the night before. He was dizzy and weak. Dr. Michaels immediately started Billy on IV fluids. She had her nurse draw labs and take his vitals. Billy had a temperature of 102. Dr. Michaels wanted him admitted immediately to treat his neutropenic fever. Her nurse called up to the bone marrow transplant unit and asked if they had a room available. Dr. Michaels and Dr. Folley, the Director of the Bone Marrow Unit, agreed that Billy would benefit from a trial stay in the bone marrow unit before his transplant. They wanted him to get familiar with the unit and the staff, and this admission was an opportunity to fulfill that request. Billy's room wasn't ready until later in the afternoon, but the nursing staff made Billy as comfortable as possible, pushing the desk up against the examination bed to lengthen it for him. We found a few extra pillows and blankets and kept him snuggled and warm.

Two different antibiotics were run through the port, and a bolus of Kytril and Demerol were administered. When we went up to the bone marrow unit, we were greeted by the clinical director, who gave me a quick tour, while Dr. Folley spoke with Billy. Both Billy and I were amazed at how incredible the unit was. Everything was new and clean. The nurses and staff physicians were so thorough and very nice. The sheets were a peach color, and the rooms were large, furnished with a desk, two side chairs, a full-length mirror, a faux leather reclining chair, full closet, and a private shower. The unit resident stays in private quarters, and there was a family lounge, family kitchen complete with an oven, sink, refrigerator, and conference room. There was also a social worker on staff who met with each family in the unit, and she assessed each of their individual needs.

The doctor and I reviewed all Billy's medications, and since he wasn't able to swallow anything because of his throat infection, they converted his oral medications to IV, except for the Marinol. There was no intravenous substitution for that. They had to infuse two pints of blood. His hemoglobin was down to seven. Billy was tired and still in great pain. The nurses were very informative. They advised me that neutropenic fevers were not that uncommon, but they could be fatal if antibiotics were not administered immediately. They said Billy would feel better within a couple of hours.

The bone marrow unit was a sterile environment, and patients and visitors alike had to follow sterile guidelines. When entering the unit, there was a sterile air chamber where you donned sterile gowns, washed your hands, and applied disposable gloves. If the patient was quarantined due to an infection or low blood counts, visitors were required to wear masks. The patient's safety was first and foremost in the bone marrow transplant unit. The patients were encouraged to walk the halls within the unit and interact with the other BMT (Bone Marrow Transplant) patients, when they were feeling up to it. If patients had a fever or infection, they were quarantined to their rooms, however, for their safety, as well as the safety of the other patients.

Billy was happy to be in the unit. He felt at ease there, and he told me he was fine there and I didn't have to stay the night. He thought I should take the boys home and get a good night's sleep. I was hesitant to leave him with a fever. The nurses again told me that the patients were given ultimate care and encouraged me to leave. They said they would call me immediately if there were any developments or if an emergency arose. I told Billy I would go home for one night and if he needed me or if he did not show improvement, I would stay the next.

It turned out he needed platelets the next day, and his infection was not clearing up. The doctor approached me as I entered the unit the next day and told me how uncomfortable he was with the fact that Billy had a neutropenic fever at this time in his therapy and he couldn't understand why the infection was so bad this time. He did find bacteria in the cultures the lab technician had drawn. I asked the doctor if bacteria was found in the port or in the peripheral cultures, and he said he honestly did not remember. He said Billy was on a regimen of prophylactic antibiotics, not specific for the infection and the team wanted to run more tests to identify the bacteria. He felt it might have been viral. He said he would call the urologist to review Billy's chart and also to have an ultrasound performed on the kidneys. He noted that Dr. Michaels was very stringent on starting Billy's chemotherapy on the twenty-first day. He questioned whether she waited until the platelet counts were up. I told him she always waited for the counts to go up. It was usually like clockwork. The counts went up on a Thursday, and he was back in the hospital on a Monday. The doctor was relieved to learn she did wait for the counts. He said it wasn't that unusual with Billy's protocol and it was permissible to start the next cycle on day twenty-one, even if platelets were a little below one hundred. Nevertheless, he had us wait to see what the numbers were before he let Dr. Michaels make the call. I told him Billy was scheduled for the pulmonary function test on Thursday, April 8, 1998, and he said Billy was fine for that. He also arranged for the CT scan and the other tests he deemed necessary before Billy was discharged. He felt it was much easier for Billy to get it all done while he was in the hospital rather than make him return for various tests.

Billy's fever escalated to 103, and they drew blood cultures to ascertain they were at the proper levels of antibiotics (gentamicin, vancomycin, acyclovir). I was given a blood-count log and a pamphlet so I could keep track of his counts myself. I was impressed that the nurses in this unit were more than willing to help teach, inform, and assist both the patient and his family with any and all of the patient's care while in the unit.

On April 7, 1998, Billy had to undergo a stent-replacement surgery. The surgery was about forty-five minutes, and the urologist said Billy tolerated the procedure well. He allowed me to stay with Billy in the recovery room. When I entered the room, Billy opened his eyes and started screaming that his rear end was burning. He said it felt like it was on fire. I called the nurse over to examine him, and she found his bottom to be extremely red and irritated. It appeared he had had some sort of an adverse reaction to the Betadine solution used during the surgery. They administered ice and then Silvadene cream.

After about a half-hour, Billy felt some relief. He was experiencing a very dry mouth, and he was drifting in and out of consciousness. I stayed with him until the nurses brought him back to his room. As the anesthesia began to wear off, the nurses gave him Ativan and Kytril through his IV line to calm him down, as he was still complaining about his bottom. He was angry and uncomfortable, and I just wanted him to be able to sleep. After all the procedures he had gone through, never once had Billy reacted to Betadine solution. We couldn't figure out how or why this reaction occurred this time. The doctors could not come up with any explanation as to what was different in that operating room than any other surgery he had undergone. It had remained an unsolved mystery.

Finally, a week after Billy was admitted to the bone marrow unit, the doctors had written the discharge orders, and I brought Billy home. Billy was glad to be home, despite the fact it was a cold, rainy, miserable day. He didn't eat much and had a hard time sleeping. We continued with the TPN at night, and Billy would take naps during the day. He tried to stop at the stone yard for at least an hour or two during the day for something to do, and if he felt up to it, he would wash the car or take a ride with one of the drivers. Since Easter was fast approaching, I did my baking and shopping chores. We had everyone at our house for Easter dinner, and Billy was happy to celebrate a holiday home with all of our family. It was the first time in many years that all of my brothers and their children were together in town for a holiday dinner. We had tables and chairs set from wall to wall, but it was wonderful. Dinner was from soup to nuts, and desserts were too many to mention. Kevin stopped by to see Billy before dinner, and later they played N64 games. Billy was exhausted and fell asleep around eleven o'clock in the evening.

A few weeks later, Nicole had acute appendicitis, and Billy thought it ironic that he was the one visiting the patient for once. She was in the hospital three days, and on the second day, Billy's cousin Joshua went to the hospital with Billy, and they spent the entire day visiting Nicole. They had fun talking and joking with her. Mom and I went after work, and we sent the boys to Wawa this time to get Nicole the Gatorade and chicken noodle soup. We laughed now that the tables were turned. Billy was happy to be on the other side of the hospital bed for once. On the day Nicole was discharged, Billy brought her home. We were teasing them both and said that patient number one was bringing home patient number two to Rainey Rehab. I worked a half-day and prepared a nice lunch for the two of them and tried to keep her as comfortable as possible.

Her sorority was having a pasta dinner fundraiser that night for Billy, and she had every intention of attending. Even though she was not up to working in the kitchen, she did not want to miss the special function in honor of her brother. She went and supervised and watched in awe as the college students streamed in to support this most worthy cause so close to her heart. Aunt JoAnne and Joshua even attended in support of Billy. He was overwhelmed at their kindness and the generosity of so many, even that of strangers.

During the course of the next few days, Billy went to the yard and tried to do a few things within his strength capacity. On some days he went on deliveries with Matt, and other days he stayed at the yard and assisted customers with their orders. Although he did not have the strength to lift the heavy bags of mulch or soil, occasionally he would operate the forklift or the Bobcat. He knew his limits and was very careful. When he was fatigued, he would go home and nap. I was glad he had some stamina and he was home, as I had to assist Nicole at school. She had a couple of classes she wanted to make up from her surgery, and she was still weak from surgery and unable to drive.

On Billy's nineteenth birthday, he wasn't feeling well but tolerable enough to go to the yard. He helped out in the office for a few hours, and Nicole stopped there to spend more time with him before going to the house for dinner, as she had class later that evening. Billy requested pizza for dinner. It was quick and easy, and he wanted to take his brothers, Matthew and Sean, to Atco Raceway that evening. Though he only drove in one race, he won. He enjoyed it immensely. He met his friend Matt there, as well as his cousin, Joshua and some of his friends. They all had a fantastic time. We had cake and opened presents when they returned home. The boys gave Billy his initial ring, and we all gave him money. He was pleased with his gifts and so very grateful he was able to get to Atco, and very pleased that he won, as he was scheduled for his final round of chemotherapy the next morning. Billy knew what was ahead of him. Therefore, he wanted to participate in as many fun-filled activities as possible prior to round seven.

Round Seven

On April 29, 1998, the day after Billy's birthday, he was admitted at one o'clock in the afternoon on three east. We tried to get his room changed, as we requested, to three west, but we were told there were no rooms available on three west. However, I must say, everyone had gone out of their way to make our stay comfortable that time. I suppose they were all made aware of our last visit on three east that was such a disaster. Once again, they had not started the chemotherapy on time, and while he waited, he paced the floors back and forth from the hall to his room, and it was a good thing. Billy had noticed an orange bag hanging in the closet, and he brought it to my attention. We both knew from the color it was Adriamycin, which was not scheduled for cycle seven. I asked the charge nurse on duty to call Dr. Michaels's office and question the bag of Adriamycin in his medicine closet. When Dr. Michaels called back to our room, she apologized, telling us she miscounted the cycles and thought it was cycle six. She said she had to rewrite the chemotherapy orders, and the medicine would be sent up to our room shortly. Two hours later, Dr. Michaels went to Billy's room and again apologized for the mix-up. I told her we still did not have the chemotherapy orders and Billy was still waiting for the medicine to be administered. She advised that it took two hours for the pharmacy to prepare the orders, assuming they received the orders when she submitted them. She tried to assure me that everything was fine and under control and told me to just relax.

I explained to her that everything was not fine. Billy was made to wait for his chemotherapy to start on more than one occasion, and there were too many mistakes to mention. I reminded her of several of the mistakes that had occurred while we were in the hospital and said that if Billy and I were not our own advocates of his care, who knew what catastrophic things could have happened. I reminded her of nursing mistakes, physician mistakes, and pharmacy mistakes. I also reminded her that I was still awaiting copies of reports from April 14. She asked if I could please go to her office on Friday to get these copies, as she wanted to be with me to go over everything personally, and she was too busy on Thursday. I agreed, and we parted on that note. I returned to Billy's room and waited patiently for the chemotherapy to begin.

When we met on Friday, Dr. Michaels apologized for all of the conflicts we had encountered during our treatment sessions. She explained that this was a hard time for us and that families generally deal with stress and illness differently and said Billy and I seemed to be extremely on top of things. She mentioned that I, in particular, liked to be in control of things. I agreed with her on that point, especially when it came to my son. I certainly did like to be in control, and control was one thing I did not have over his disease. We were fighting against all odds, and we were frustrated and running into brick walls. I reminded her of Billy's scholarship to Pennco Tech. He had already missed the first semester of school, and the sooner we completed the P6 protocol, the sooner he could get on with his life. I explained that all my son wanted was to get back to some sort of a natural lifestyle.

At this point, I really did believe we were going to beat this thing. Billy had so many good days. He had strength within to give this a good fight. He had been through so much so far. He would be the one breakthrough in the research. He would make it. Yet I thought there were too many mistakes for such a high-ranking hospital system. I mentioned our concerns that she was not giving us enough information, that she did not spend enough time on details, and that she was not always prepared to answer our questions. We realized this was a newly diagnosed disease and she wanted to be certain before she gave us information, but it seemed we always had to request things a number of times before we received them. I also brought up alternate treatment plans such as sharks cartilage, vitamins, MSN, and the Livingston Institute in California. Dr. Michaels said she felt the P6 protocol was the only proven program for this particular cancer. She said, "This is the only one proven to work, or at least the only proven one that gets results." She further stated, "It's our only chance." And said she knew people all over the world and had done research on this and there were people who would prey on cancer patients and their families. So far, the P6 was what she endorsed.

She said we could supplement Billy's diet with vitamin E and vitamin C in addition to his treatment plan. She then suggested we have the second-look surgery at the end of May and the bone marrow transplant by mid-July, followed by radiation therapy in September or October. She thought it might be best if Billy waited to enroll in school until the next January. She promised to make a point of being better prepared and more informative in the future. I relayed this information to Billy, and he hoped to see an improvement in both his health and Dr. Michaels's preparedness. I told Dr. Michaels of another patient we heard mention of who had been treating with Dr. Kushner along with a doctor from Jefferson for the diagnosis of DSRCT. Dr. Michaels denied any knowledge of another patient with the same diagnosis as Billy at Jefferson, but promised to look into it. Whether or not she ever did, we will never know.

Regardless, Billy met that patient, Bob McCarthy on April 30, 1998, at Jefferson Hospital. He was twenty-seven years old and diagnosed with DSRCT in November of 1997, one month after Billy was diagnosed. Bob did not undergo surgery. He started immediately with chemotherapy, from which he lost most of his hearing. He was wearing a hearing aid now and asked if Billy experienced any hearing loss. Fortunately, Billy escaped that one. Bob started his seventh cycle of chemotherapy the same week as Billy, and he had been conferring with Dr. Kushner in New York as well. This was his last day of therapy, and he was being discharged. Billy was sorry he did not meet him sooner, but they exchanged contact information and knew they would keep in touch. I wanted to meet Bob's mother and hoped to run into her before his discharge. (Coincidentally, Billy and I did continue to see Bob at Sloan-Kettering on several occasions.)

This round of chemotherapy consisted of ifosfamide and etoposide, both of which were administered by one-hour infusions over five days. Mesna was also administered by intravenous injection with the cyclophosphamide to prevent bleeding in the bladder and kidneys. And again, ten days after the completion of the course when his blood cell count was down, I had to inject the GCSF injections, a blood cell growth stimulant.

Billy was unusually tired during this round of chemotherapy. He would either sleep right through breakfast or would awaken just to eat and fall back asleep until the next meal arrived. When the nurses went into the room for vitals or medications, he would sleep right through their rounds. Since most of the medications were injected through his IV line, it was no problem for him to sleep through it. In the evenings, though, after dinner, Billy and I continued to watch movies.

The Eucharistic minister continued to bring communion to Billy, and I would go to St. John's for mass. I was comforted by the opened arms of Padre Pio's life-size statue in the lower level of the most beautifully architecturally structured building in the city with spectacular stained-glass windows. After mass, I would kneel at the feet of Padre Pio and stare into his eyes as I prayed, and then I would read the inscription below:

> Pray, hope and don't worry. Worry is useless.
>
> God is merciful and will hear your prayers.
>
> Padre Pio

When Billy had a good day, I would go to the office for a few hours and return to the hospital at lunchtime. If he was feeling okay, I would return to the office. But, if he was having pain or feeling depressed, I would call the office and stay with Billy for the rest of the day. I was very fortunate to have such an understanding firm that worked with me during that time. They were completely supportive and behind me all the way. They allowed me to work from the New Jersey office when Billy was home and in the Philadelphia office when he was in the hospital. If there was work that absolutely needed to be done, I would either bring a Dictaphone to the hospital and type it on my laptop, save it on a disk and print it at the office the next day, or I would ask someone at the office to print it. Usually it was not an issue and I was able to complete the task myself. Billy understood that I needed to get my work done, and it never took me too long to complete a task, so I would run to the office and do the rush task and return to the hospital to be with him.

On the sixth day, Billy was finally discharged. He was so glad to finally be home. He felt relieved to be finished with the chemotherapy portion of the P6 protocol. We both felt as though we were one step closer to the finish line. Ryan went to the house right on schedule the day after Billy's discharge and accessed Billy's port. As usual, he drew his labs and made sure I had enough supplies to run the TPN starting immediately that night, and the Neupogen and Epogen in a few days, as soon as Billy's counts dropped. Both Billy and I couldn't wait until the day came when I wouldn't have to stick him with needles anymore. That is one of the most horrible things a mom has to do to her son. It was bad enough he had to get needles, but to get them from his mom! It wasn't long before Dr. Michaels called; Billy's white and red counts were low. I had to start the Neupogen as well as the Epogen injections. Two needles was a lot to handle at once, but we got through it. Billy was a trooper.

We were now in the month of May, and it was a very busy month. Sean was making his Confirmation, and Billy was his sponsor. Nicole was graduating from Rutgers University, and we were planning a graduation party, and Billy was excited to be a part of the planning. He kept busy getting the yard landscaped and helping Nicole coordinate the party arrangements. One day after working at the yard in the morning, he mowed the lawn and was so tired afterward, he slept until dinner. I asked him to wait for another day to cut the grass, but he wouldn't give in to the fatigue. He was strong willed to continue his pre-cancer life-style as much as possible. It just wasn't in him to put things off until another day. If he started a job, he wanted to finish it, and if something needed to be done, he did it.

On the night of Sean's confirmation, Billy's counts were down to a dangerously low 1.0, but he was determined to stand for Sean regardless. It was a beautiful ceremony, and Billy miraculously made it through the mass despite the low blood cell counts. I was a bit worried that he was in the midst of a large crowd of people, so we did hurry out of church afterward and had cake and desserts back at our house. Billy visited with Kevin for about an hour later in the evening, and then I had to administer his Neupogen injection and his TPN before he went to bed. It was an exhausting evening for all of us, but Billy did have a good night's sleep.

The following day, Ryan took Billy's labs and later called to say that his platelet counts were low and they would affect the barium enema he had scheduled. He advised that we call the hospital in the morning and ask whether we should postpone the test until his counts improved. Dr. Michaels's office also called and reported that Billy's platelet counts were 37,000, and they should be at least 50,000. They wanted Billy to go to the hospital the following Monday for more labs to be drawn. If the lab work results were within normal limits, then it would be okay for Billy to proceed with the barium enema. In the meantime, since we had to postpone the barium enema, we had to in turn postpone the CT scan, as that couldn't be completed until after the barium enema was done to clear his system.

After Billy's blood test, he went to the stone yard to borrow his friend Matt's trailer so he could bring his bike to his Aunt JoAnne's on the trailer. He and Josh rode in the woods behind Aunt JoAnne's house, Billy on his dirt bike and Josh on the quad. JoAnne and I were a nervous wreck the whole time the boys were riding, but the boys enjoyed themselves immensely. It was an afternoon Joshua and JoAnne will never forget. Billy said it was the best afternoon he had had in months.

Billy remained busy the next few days before his barium enema. He put the fog lights on the Altima, and he continued to go to the stone yard for a few hours each day. He knew once he had the barium enema he wouldn't have any strength.

As he predicted, the barium enema was extremely awful. It left Billy in so much pain. We had to follow up with Dr. Berber. While waiting in her office, we met Bob McCarthy and his mother. I introduced myself to her, and we spoke briefly about our sons' histories. Both sons were following Dr. Kushner's protocol. Rob, however, had been receiving his radiation treatments at Memorial Sloan-Kettering rather than at Jefferson. He was seeing Dr. Berber at this time for the hip aspiration. They were checking to make sure there was no cancer in his bone marrow. He had not yet had the stem cell collection.

This was Billy's pre-surgical visit with Dr. Berber. He had blood drawn, and he had to have a Sigmoid Flux. She also went over the results of the barium enema and the blood tests done the week prior. She wanted to make sure his counts were in the proper range prior to subjecting him to surgery.

All the pretests were done, and Billy was starting to pick up a little bit of energy. He was happy to have a few days free prior to his second-look surgery. He was anxious to have enough stamina for his sister's upcoming party. Billy did so much work in preparation for it. We had rented a canopy and a dance floor, and it was a fantastic party. All the out-of-town relatives went for a double purpose, first to congratulate Nicole, and secondly to wish Billy well with his second big surgery. Billy was grateful to see everyone and graciously accepted their prayers and good wishes. The day after the party, many of our friends and family came back to our house to pray the rosary for a successful surgery scheduled the following day. We prayed for the strength to deal with whatever was ahead of us.

Second-Look Surgery

On May 27, 1998, we reported to room 9410 at twelve fifteen in the afternoon for the second-look surgery. The operative report entitled this a laparotomy, splenectomy, ileostomy closure, tumor debulking. The nurse took blood work around twelve forty-five and told us they were backed up and that Billy would most likely not get into the OR until maybe two or three o'clock in the afternoon. I then called our support team at home (mom, JoAnne, Billy's boss, Bob, and his wife, Maureen), who were all planning to wait with me on intervals at the hospital since the operation was to take several hours.

In the meantime, I waited with Billy, and we prayed the Lord's Prayer and recited various novenas. Billy said how happy he would be once the ileostomy was removed; he just couldn't wait for that to happen. That was all he could speak of, all he thought about. Of all that he had been through, the biggest obstacle he had overcome as a young man was the ileostomy. It was just one of those things that a young man didn't want to deal with. It is something that most of us wouldn't want to deal with, young or old, male or female. It isn't an easy task to accomplish, and it is not the way things are supposed to work. We also spoke about how far he had come in his therapy and how well the doctors felt he had tolerated the chemotherapy. We both were hoping for a positive report from the surgeon and looking forward to seeing an end to this long journey. We continued to pray and knew our prayers would be heard.

Finally, at six o'clock in the evening, Billy was called back to the holding area, and I was permitted to stay until they administered the IV medications. I kissed him one last time, and the nurse and the anesthesiologist rolled his gurney through the automatic doors. As the doors closed, I called out to him that I loved him and everything would be fine. I said I would be there as soon as they would let me see him, and then the doors closed. As I wiped the tears from my eyes, I met up with my mother, Bill and the kids, Nicole, Matthew, and Sean; then my sister JoAnne and Joshua.

We registered with the receptionist on the eighth-floor waiting area and then went for a quick bite to eat. When we returned to the waiting area, we were advised that they would be closing at eight o'clock and we would have to move to the seventh floor. When we arrived on the seventh floor, we again registered with the volunteer there and were greeted by Bob and Maureen. Then Kevin anxiously arrived, waiting for some results. Everyone was talking around me. I was hearing them but not listening to a word they were saying. My mind was racing. I continued to pray and think of how long it was taking and how I wanted to be with my son. Why weren't they calling me in? When would I be able to see my son? Was he all right? Were they able to reverse the ileostomy? Had the chemotherapy significantly reduced the tumor? Were we able to continue the protocol safely? Was Billy in remission yet? I could only hope for a miracle. Were our prayers answered? Was my baby saved? I didn't hear a thing. I couldn't sit still. I had to get up. I began to pace the floor, and then I started to walk a little farther, starting out the door and down the hall, afraid to wander too far from earshot of the waiting area phone. I wanted to be sure I heard the phone ring and heard my name, should they call it. While I was wandering up the hall, Dr. Berber turned the corner and walked toward me. I hurriedly walked closer to her, anxious to hear what she had to say.

"Is Billy all right? Can I see him? Were you able to reverse the ileostomy?" I fired so many questions to her she didn't have a chance to get a word in.

When I stopped long enough to catch my breath, the doctor told me the surgery went well. She said they were able to remove a lot of tumor residual that melted away from the chemotherapy. The liver looked good, as did the bladder and kidneys. The diaphragm, on the other hand, was more involved with disease. Radiation, at that juncture, was not an option but more of a necessity. Then the news came that literally knocked me to my knees. I collapsed and fell to the floor as the words exited the doctor's mouth: "We were not able to reverse the ileostomy."

My mother and sister ran to my side as soon as they saw me fall to the floor. They pulled me to my feet and held me in their arms as I cried, "They couldn't reverse the ileostomy. They couldn't reverse the ileostomy. Oh, my God. What am I going to tell Billy?" The stinging words of the doctor echoed in my head. There was no way I could relay this information to my son. This was all he had asked from the surgery. He wanted to get rid of the bag. His words resounded: "I can't wait to get rid of this ileostomy. If they can't reverse it, don't even wake me up from the operation, Mom." I knew Billy didn't really mean that. Nevertheless, I know he didn't want to wake up with the bag still attached to his abdomen. He was anxiously awaiting this surgery, anticipating the reversal of the ileostomy, and he expected nothing less from the surgery. Now it was I who had to relay the earth shattering news to my son, and I wasn't sure I could pull the task off. I didn't have any strength left. I was a hollow shell. I could barely walk without the assistance of my mother and sister. How could I pretend to tell my son it was okay to live with an ileostomy bag at the age of nineteen? It just wasn't right. It wasn't fair.

Dr. Berber said she did not tell Billy about the ileostomy. She said he did not ask, and she would see him the following day. I was worried and concerned as to how I was going to tell him. I was unsure how he was going to handle the news of the ileostomy being permanent and something that could no longer be reversed. Dr. Berber said she would give him all the medical details when she spoke with him, but I knew he would not want to hear all of that. He just wanted to be free of the bag, and that was that.

I was permitted to go into the recovery room at eleven thirty to be with Billy. He was just coming out of the anesthesia and was very uncomfortable. He appeared to be in great pain. I was able to hold him and comfort him for a while. A nurse administered some pain medicine, and he fell in and out of sleep for about a half hour. Around midnight, when Billy awakened, he stared at me with his beautiful brown eyes and asked me if the bag was gone. I blinked back tears, and before I could answer him, he asked a second time, "Mom, did they reverse the ileostomy?"

"Oh, Billy, no. Dr. Berber said it was too difficult to reverse. There were too many complications, and she will have to talk to you about it tomorrow. I am so sorry, honey."

"*No!*" he screamed out in disbelief. It was too much for me to cope with. The two of us just cried. I held him as close to me as I could. He had so many apparatuses connected to him it was difficult to hold him. I held his hands and rested my head on his chest. I couldn't bear to see my son in so much pain. No mother should ever have to see her child suffer so—never, never. This was beyond anything anyone could ever believe. Billy was so upset. His heart rate was over one-hundred fifty. The nurse tried to get it down. We stayed in the PACU until eight o'clock in the morning, monitoring him until it finally went down to one thirty. There was no way I could ever leave his side at this point, not after he had suffered this emotional trauma. He was so sure he was going to be free of his ileostomy, and then to learn otherwise—I couldn't leave him alone in his depression.

In addition to his disappointment of the ileostomy, Billy had experienced extreme pain as a result of the surgery. The epidural catheter had been discontinued, and the morphine was causing him severe itching reaction, so they switched to Dilaudid. That didn't prove to be very effective for Billy, so the pain-management team decided to try the epidural again and fentanyl, giving him some pain relief, but it was only temporary. The next few nights proved to be rough for Billy. One night we had pain management come in to the room every hour on the hour, and they still could not control his pain. In addition to being in pain, whenever the nurses went in to take his blood pressure, the IV in his hands would bleed and start to leak fluid, which caused more pain for Billy.

I was frustrated at the poor management of Billy's pain and sternly reminded the doctors that he had the port and since we had tried everything else, it was time to take advantage of the port for his pain management. One doctor spoke to another, and finally they agreed. There was one small factor: the nurses didn't feel comfortable accessing the port. We waited for the nursing supervisor to come from the third floor to show the nurses how to access Billy's port for his pain medications. Once it was finally done, Billy was so much more comfortable.

Once Billy was feeling better, Dr. Berber was able to answer all of our questions about the surgery. She explained to Billy how they tried for two hours to separate the bladder from the rectum and that the dangerous outcome of this could have resulted in bladder incontinence as well as bowel incontinence. She didn't think Billy would have appreciated the loss of control of his bowel and bladder just to have the ostomy bag removed. Billy was quiet as she spoke. He just listened and absorbed everything as she continued. There was a lot of scar tissue. She said scar tissue fuses immediately after surgery. She said these areas were clearly not visible on the barium enema or sigmoid flux. She said she was disappointed that they were unsuccessful in reversing the ileostomy, but she was pleased that they were able to clear the abdomen of any tumor. She explained that they outlined the diaphragm with a metallic substance so the radiologist would be able to identify the tumor for radiation.

It took a few more days before Billy's pain became manageable and he was able to keep down more than clear foods. He was anxious to go home, but the doctors and staff wanted to take it slow and make sure his counts were within normal limits and he could be weaned off the pain medications. Once they disconnected the PCA pump and his pain was under control, Billy began to eat better, and the doctors felt he could be discharged. By the second day of June, just six days after surgery, Billy was able to go home.

Billy slept a little better once at home, and his appetite improved. On the second day home, he took the car out to the mall to get Kevin a birthday present. Billy and I were aware the discharge papers indicated he wasn't to drive for another week, but he insisted on driving, expressing he was more relaxed and in less pain when he drove. After all he had been through, I wasn't going to argue with him, and besides, the mall was only a few blocks away. A few days later, though, he drove again, this time a little farther, taking his brother Matthew to Atco and then to a movie. He said he was tired of lying around and wanted to keep as busy as possible. My heart was breaking for my son; I couldn't restrict him to the house. He was gaining strength day by day and promised he would call me immediately if he felt tired or wasn't up to driving home. I wasn't about to quarrel with him over a matter of days. I thought that was the best thing for him at the time. After all, keeping him busy seemed to get his mind off his pain. He did appear to be eating better, and he was sleeping better at night. I did worry, though, when he and Kevin spent

explaining what had been going on the past few days, and, of course, I had to bring him into the ER.

The ER started an IV with fluids, Zofran, and antibiotics. His counts showed some sort of infection. His hemoglobin was fine. He didn't appear to lose much blood. The resident ordered X-rays, which were inconclusive. He was transferred to a room on the fifth floor, and he was monitored closely over a twenty-four hour period. I went home to gather some things for both Billy and myself and then brought Matthew to mass, after which I took a bath and then ran back to the hospital. The evening nurse alerted security that I would be returning after hours and had reserved a cot for me in Billy's room. They were so accommodating on the fifth floor. Billy's stomach had calmed down, and he was feeling much better after the fluids and medications. We watched the Phillies and Cubs game together until we fell asleep. It had been another long day for the two of us.

We were awakened around four thirty in the morning by the clanking of the nurse's cart. She had come to hang a unit of blood. Billy's hemoglobin had dropped to nine from thirteen the previous day. He was running a low-grade fever. She asked him if he wanted a Tylenol suppository, but he refused. A gastroenterologist went in to speak with Billy about doing an endoscopy. Billy didn't want the test, but the doctor said he wanted to get to the bottom of the vomiting and nausea, and the lower-GI tests were relatively clear. We were wondering if the bouncing in the truck played a factor in his nausea. The doctor didn't think so, but I disagreed. Unless it was coincidental. The last time Billy got sick, he was in the truck with Matt on a Thursday and got sick on Friday. This week Billy was in the truck on Friday, and he went to the hospital on Saturday. I though it might have been worth looking into. The doctor consulted with two others, and the endoscopy was their only hope for answers at that juncture, so it was scheduled. Billy was not happy, but he conceded.

Nicole and Kevin went to the hospital and tried to lift Billy's spirits, as he was more than a bit down. He was even getting a little grouchy at that point. He wanted to eat, drink, play, and get out of the hospital. We took Billy for a walk and sat in the lounge for a little while. Nicole and Kevin had him laughing. It was good seeing him interact with them at such a hard time in his life. His spirits were lifted, if even for a little while, and I thanked God for that. I thanked his brothers and sister and Kevin every day for all they had done for Billy. It made all the difference in the world.

Billy had the endoscopy the next day. Surprisingly, the procedure was not painful for him. He came out of the anesthesia in good spirits. He was feeling great. He was only allowed clears at first, but he finished everything off the lunch and dinner trays. We walked down to the lounge area again and bought a cup of chicken broth for the two of us. He was really hungry and still in a great mood. We watched TV together, took another walk, and talked a lot. It was Matthew's birthday, Mom and Bob went to our house since Nicole had an ice cream cake for him. They called over the phone so Billy and I could join in and sing "Happy Birthday" to Matthew. Bittersweet, I know. We tried as much as possible to be a part of everything at home.

Billy was discharged a few days later, after he proved he could tolerate a regular diet. He was happy to be home. One of the first things he did was take Matthew to a Phillies game for a belated birthday gift. A few days later, he took Sean to one of his little league games, and then he went shopping with Nicole. He didn't want another minute to pass him by. He tried to capture as many moments as he could with his siblings. One evening we sat around the dining room table and played Harley Davidson Monopoly. Billy missed being home together with the family, and he treasured what little time he had between hospital stays. I knew it was hard for Billy, not knowing when he would have an issue with his stomach or when his hemoglobin counts would drop again, but I assured him he was not alone. I was right there by his side through it all. We all were.

Cruise to Nowhere

On July 3, 1998, we sailed from New York City aboard a cruise ship at four thirty in the afternoon for a weekend cruise to nowhere with the family and, of course, Kevin. After all, being Billy's best friend, he was part of the family. The kids had a great stateroom with a double window; our cabin was a bit smaller, and we were very close to the disco. The view was spectacular. It was our first time on a cruise, and it was Kevin's first time to see Liberty Island, the Statue of Liberty, and Ellis Island. I also think the boys were first in line for the casinos. Of course, they were first in line to get a Bahama Mama and their souvenir cup. Being out at sea, we were on maritime law, and Billy and Kevin were over eighteen. There was food constantly, from soup to nuts for breakfast, lunch, and dinner, or practically around the clock, and all the desserts one could ever dream of. There were fireworks on Saturday night, discos and deck parties, pool parties, midnight buffets, and various activities during the day. We tried our hand at simulated horseracing, shuffleboard, and I actually enjoyed relaxing by the pool. I believe there was a movie showing in the evening, but the boys were not interested, and no one found the Bingo tables too amusing.

There was one particular event that piqued their interest, and that was a talent show. Guests were asked to dress in drag with props from whatever their team had with them. The participants were great sports and very entertaining. The show was hilarious, and prizes were awarded. Our team won! We could not have asked for a more perfect weekend, everyone had so much fun. We truly enjoyed ourselves, and I was sorry I did not book a longer cruise. We all could have used more time to relax. It was so difficult going back to reality and doctor appointments, blood tests and hospital visits. A few days after we returned home, we met with Dr. Michaels and discussed our next phase of the protocol. The bone marrow transplant unit had tentatively scheduled the transplant for July 28, 1998. Dr. Michaels proposed Billy's admission on July 19 for six days of chemotherapy and two days of rest and then begin the stem cell infusion on the twenty-eighth. This required the stents be changed prior to the transplant, and Billy was scheduled to visit urology immediately after our visit with Dr. Michaels.

The days leading to his admission to the bone marrow transplant unit, Billy continued to feel great. He went down the shore with Kevin, and his uncle took them fishing. After catching a flounder, a dolphin went up to their boat. They were so excited to have had the chance to be so close to a dolphin, not to mention the fact that they had the opportunity to pet and feed it. Of course, no one had a camera. But this was one of those moments when a camera was not needed. Neither the boys nor Kevin's uncle John would ever forget. I too was grateful that Billy had the memory to share with us when he returned home. He also brought home the fresh fillets and individually wrapped flounder, which Billy was proud to cook on the grill throughout the summer.

Billy kept himself busy during the rest of the summer, riding his dirt bike with Matt and Josh. A few times he would even borrow Matt's trailer to hitch his dirt bike to his car so he could drive down to Josh's to ride bikes in the woods. My sister JoAnne would be so nervous, but she would always take pictures whenever they were within sight racing by on their bikes. Despite our pleas of caution, they were still nineteen-year-old boys without a sense of fear and a little bit of daredevil in their blood. Luckily they scathed through their adventures without incidents or injuries. On one occasion, Billy and Josh even had enough energy after a day of riding to sit through a late show at the movie theater.

Billy wanted to spend as much time as possible enjoying the outdoors. He would take Matthew and Sean fishing at Cooper River, where they would sometimes get catfish and sunnies on the end of their lines. One afternoon I joined the boys on their outing, and after climbing over several hundred feet of uneven trail scattered with various rocks, I found a tree trunk to sit on. "Aw, c'mon, Mom, you tired already?" asked Matthew. "We haven't been walking that far." Not far for the supercharged boys I was trailing behind. They were having a ball, romping ahead of me over stumps and boulders, while I was tangled between tree roots.

"Wanna rest for a while, Mom?" said Billy. "We can stop here. Matt, Sean, let's sit here in the shade for a minute."

We sat in an area shaded by various pine trees, oaks, and a few cedars overlooking murky, brown water. The boys gathered a few pebbles and began tossing them across the water, forming a ripple effect. Mesmerized by the small waves in the water, I decided I would try my hand at tossing a few stones. Only, when I threw the first stone in, it just plunked directly into the water without a ripple, so I tried it again. The boys laughed. I tried it a third time, this time with a gentle twist of my wrist, and again the stone dropped directly to the bottom of the muddy water. Matthew and Billy each rushed to my side with a pebble and said in unison, "Mom, watch me, this is how you do it." Each demonstrated his own technique and step-by-step instructions of how to throw the perfect skipping stone while Sean gave me a gentle hug and told me not to feel bad. He said it was all right, and later they brought me a supply of pebbles. I tried to copy the body language of both Matthew and Billy while releasing the first pebble into the water. My release was a bit awkward, but there was a slight ripple. They repeated the lesson until I learned how to skip stones, and then I became almost as good as the boys—okay, not really, but not bad for a rookie. We sat, talked, and laughed while we continued skipping stones, reminiscing about our mini cruise and past summer vacations, and though we had some memorable vacations, most of our special moments happened to be extraordinary segments of ordinary days, just like this one.

The Bone Marrow Transplant

T he day for Billy's bone marrow transplant had come. He
was admitted to Jefferson University Hospital on July
21, 1998, at ten o'clock in the morning. That was the
only part of Billy's treatment where they did not allow me to stay
at the hospital, not in the beginning, anyway. I was emotionally
torn, not being by my son's side during that time. I was not sure
how he was going to react to the nursing staff without me at the
hospital, but he was a trooper, and the staff was great. I stayed
until ten or eleven o'clock at night, and if a problem arose, I was
less than a half-hour drive away, and Billy knew he could call me
at any time.

The nurse accessed his port at eleven o'clock in the morning
and recorded his vital signs. His labs were drawn, both blood
and urine. They checked his CBC levels before administering
the next chemotherapy drug, thiotepa, and checked his creatinine levels before administering the carboplatin. An EKG and a
chest X-ray were taken for baseline markers. The bone marrow

transplant involved six days of chemotherapy, and two days of rest before the actual stem cell transplant.

The first day with the thiotepa went well for Billy. The nurse told him that particular medication didn't usually make patients nauseous, but it did sometimes darken their skin, similar to a suntan. Other than being a bit tired and not having much of an appetite, Billy breezed through day one. As we entered into the second day, however, he began to get nauseous, and the vomiting began by midafternoon. Billy began with Ativan and Zofran. He had very little sleep as a result of the vomiting, and the doctor added Marinol. That combination worked well, and Billy fell asleep after a dose of Marinol. He woke up in the middle of the night and asked for a snack then fell back to sleep until morning.

On the first day of the carboplatin, Sean and I went to the hospital early in the morning. Billy was very nauseous. He declined breakfast and refused to eat lunch. The nurse was disappointed that he wasn't eating but said she wasn't going to force him to eat. She said he would eat when he felt up to it. She explained to Billy how the cells were expelled from the body, saying, "You may see blood in your urine and stools, but don't worry. This is normal. This is how the cells are excreted from your body's waste. If you're not sure about something, just ask a nurse, and we'll check it out for you, okay? "

She then gave me printed information on thiotepa and carboplatin.

Later in the day when Nicole visited him, she said she was in the mood for pizza and ordered it. When the pizza arrived, Billy ate three slices within two hours. We were so thrilled to finally see him eat something.

Billy continued with the Ativan on days two and three of the carboplatin. The nurses drew his labs regularly, and the doctors said his numbers were great. They encouraged Billy to get up and walk; they said he could leave the unit if he wanted to. He could walk over the bridge to the other building or go to the atrium, whatever he wanted to do. The doctors wanted him up and around as much as possible because "the day would come when he would be confined to bed," but because he was taking so much Ativan for the nausea, he wasn't up to getting out. Luckily, though, my mother had that special knack to get him up. He even gave her a tour of the bone-marrow transplant unit. Billy had few special moments alone with his Nan. They shared hopes and fears, dreams and tears. Nan would tell Billy she would trade places with him if she could and he would always respond, "I know, Nan, I know."

Billy's appetite was scant on days two and three of the carboplatin. I spoon-fed him very little broth, and he drank some cola. He tried to taste some of his meals, but his stomach just didn't want it. He was safe with the clear liquids, and we did not want to trigger the nausea and vomiting. His numbers were good, but Billy continued to be so weak and listless; the Ativan certainly relaxed him during that first week in the BMT unit. I was thankful he was peaceful, but it was hard to accept the fact he was not eating. Billy would wake up around two or three o'clock in the afternoon and watch a movie, sit in the recliner for a few hours, and then maybe take a sip of something for dinner. If we were lucky, he would fall asleep without the Ativan. Otherwise he would get nauseous, vomit, require Ativan, and then sleep.

Once the chemotherapy cycle concluded, the nausea and vomiting cycle began. Despite the doctor's persuasion to get out of bed, even to just get in the chair, Billy was too tired and too weak to move. His medications were now converted to IV only. He couldn't have anything by mouth. He told the doctors he wasn't experiencing any pain, and they were pleased to hear that. They told Billy he was one day closer to feeling better. As long as they could take the edge off the nausea and he didn't have pain or complications, they were pleased with his progress.

On the second day of rest, Billy's counts dropped to eighteen thousand, which meant he was neutropenic and we had to wear masks when visiting him to reduce the risk of infection. Dr. Folley jokingly told Billy he didn't have to look at everybody's ugly faces now that we were wearing masks. His humor had everyone laughing, and Billy's spirits lifted. Billy would spend most of the afternoon in the lounge chair, watching two movies while I worked on the laptop, and we would spend the evenings talking about the stem cell transfusion with anxiety and apprehension. With all the literature, preparation, and information from the doctors and nurses, both Billy and I were restless and uneasy about the anticipated procedure. He ate nothing all day but a sip of Gatorade. He spit up a little, but he had no vomiting. The doctor changed the Ativan dose to one milligram every two hours around the clock rather than two milligrams every four hours; that took the edge off his pain without making him too sleepy.

Stem Cell Transfusion, July 30, 1998

The preparation time was nine thirty in the morning. Dr. Folley, a resident, two nurses, and two nursing trainees were present to assist the lab technician with the transfusion. I was permitted to stay in the room with Billy during the transfusion, as long as I followed the sterilization procedures and wore the yellow hospital gown, mask, and gloves. Holding Billy's free hand, I watched as the technician placed one bag of frozen cells in the defroster and immediately expelled it into a syringe. The nurse then injected the cells into Billy's PICC line. She flushed the line, and the process began again with the next bag.

Billy got nauseous immediately upon infusion of the first bag, and the doctor instructed the nurse to give him another dose of Ativan. After the second bag of cells was injected, Billy had to go to the bathroom. The subsequent bags of cells were uninterrupted until they used six bags of collected cells. During the procedure, the nurses placed two extra blankets over Billy, as the cells they were injecting into the PICC line were ice cold and he began to shiver. The procedure was completed much faster than I anticipated. The entire process concluded at eleven thirty-five. The nurses immediately put an overhead heat lamp on to warm Billy as he went into a peaceful sleep until the afternoon. When Billy awoke, he had a slight temperature of 99.5 and his platelets were low. He said he was starting to feel better. The nausea had subsided, but he was very tired. Platelets were infused, the Ativan continued, the TPN with no lipids were started, IV antibiotics and IV fluids were hung, and Billy went back to sleep for the night.

Billy struggled with nausea and vomiting the first week post transfusion; his platelets continued to run low, and he had a slight temperature. Billy received one or two units of platelets daily for the first nine days. Dr. Folley and I had a conference on the tenth day. He expressed his annoyance and displeasure with having any of his patients sleep through a transplant, not just Billy, but he said, given Billy's age and the fact his lungs and overall health was excellent, he was more lenient than he would be with other patients. He knew keeping Billy on enough Ativan to allow him to sleep was the only way he could combat the nausea.

I took this opportunity to ask Dr. Folley about his experience with DSRCT, and he responded that he had few transplants using this chemotherapy protocol (not specifically this type of cancer). He had, however, worked with Dr. Kushner for twelve years at Sloan-Kettering (where they saw this type of cancer more frequently). It was evident that Dr. Folley was dedicated to his work and bonded with his patients. They seemed to be more than just a case to him. He spent long hours at the hospital, and when he was in each patient's room, he never rushed out for another patient. Dr. Folley interacted well with the patients' families just as well. He made sure they knew what was happening at the time, what to expect, or what could possibly happen and ways the family could help the patient.

During our conference, Dr. Folley offered to assist us with the radiation phase once Billy was over the hump; he also recommended two radiologists when we approached that juncture. We discussed our option of going to Sloan-Kettering, as Billy and I wanted to see Dr. Kushner before we began every new phase of treatment. Dr. Folley agreed it was a wise decision. This was still very early after the transplant, and we had to see how Billy would endure this battle before we began another.

On the first three days post transfusion, Billy had a slight temperature of ninety-nine degrees and sometimes just a few points up. Platelets were administered on all three days, as his counts were below fifty. But on day four he did not need platelets—his counts were fifty-nine, and his temperature was perfect at 98.6. Subsequent days five through ten, platelets were administered. On day eleven, however, Billy's white blood cell counts had finally reached 1.2. The doctors and nurses were ecstatic. His white blood cell counts continued to rise through day nineteen, when Billy was discharged home. His white blood cell count was 9.9.

For those of you wondering why we were focusing so much on his white blood cell counts, we wiped out Billy's red blood cells and white blood cells during the transfusion. When we actually collected his stem cells, there were two lines running one at each femoral line, one collecting his blood out, the other pumping new blood in. The stem cells were collected from his blood at that time and frozen. During the transplant, the frozen stem cells were pumped into his body via a port line. This was done after high-dose chemotherapy destroyed all of his blood cells. Post the transfusion, we waited for the new cells to grow.

Billy was only home two days before the vomiting began again. It started slowly, with Billy's appetite slowing down. Then it began to increase. Billy was able to tolerate the TPN feeding at night, but he refused breakfast in the morning and didn't have much of an appetite at all by the second day. When we called Dr. Folley's assistant, she advised us to go to the BMT unit immediately. As it turned out, Billy was severely dehydrated. He was admitted once again. Once in the hospital, they were able to control the nausea, after a few hit-or-miss drugs. Haldol gave him the shakes, so they stopped that one. After trying a similar medication, which also caused an adverse reaction, the doctors listened to me and administered five milligrams of Ativan and fifty milligrams of Benadryl. Although Billy was still unable to sleep and jittery from the meds, the vomiting was finally getting under control with the Ativan. The BMT unit was so busy, and the staff was running frantically caring for other patients. Therefore Billy was discharged as soon as his symptoms dissipated. Billy was anxious to go home and tired of feeling sick. He was wondering if it was the transplant that was making him constantly nauseous.

I said, "No, honey. After all, remember all the times you would get nauseous. I'm worried now because you are getting dehydrated. You have to make sure you drink plenty of fluids."

Our conversation was interrupted with the sound of feet scurrying down the hall, followed by squeaking wheels from the medical cart. Billy and I exchanged glances, realizing the commotion was related to the complications of a fellow transplant patient. With saddened eyes, Billy asked, "Mom, did they go to Lori's room?"

Just as I tiptoed toward the door, Billy's nurse entered the room, announcing she had his bedtime cocktail of Ativan. She refreshed his water and placed it on his bed tray, humming as she handed him his medication. I interrupted her melody to ask her if Lori was okay. She replied that Lori was still fighting an infection and her fever wasn't breaking. Billy began to fumble with his hospital bracelet, staring blankly at the television. His mood became somber, and he lowered his eyes, avoiding any contact with me.

Lori was a patient in the room next to Billy's and was having complications relating to her transplant. We first noticed Lori the day Billy was admitted to the transplant unit, when she was walking down the hall with her family, trailing an IV pole. We acknowledged each other with a smile and nods. Lori's parents and I conversed frequently, keeping abreast of each other's child's progress, sharing concerns and prayers for our children. Billy felt somehow connected to Lori. They shared the same medical team, both had bone marrow transplants, and they were both fighting the odds.

After a brief silence, Billy softly said, "Mom, I hope she comes through this." Lowering his eyes he said, "I'd like to send her something. You think silk flowers would be good?"

Leaning toward him, I reached for his hand and nodded. "Ah, yes, honey. I think that would be so sweet. I could make something like I did for the office." I added, "If I can, I'll try to get to the store on my way home tonight."

"Just make sure it's something nice," he said matter of factly. "Nothing too big, but make it nice. Get a nice container, ya know, glass or something, nothing plastic."

Without saying I word, I just nodded as he continued, "Whatever. Thanks, Mom. You don't have to go right out tonight, but I was thinking maybe something to try and cheer her up, ya know."

"Sure," I said, "I'll see what I can do. I'll find something nice. Maybe I'll bring them in with me and arrange them here, I don't know. It'll be a nice display."

Before long, the combination of Ativan and Benadryl started to kick in, and Billy was fast asleep. Since this had been a particularly good day for him, I didn't feel the need to linger. I kissed him good night and headed home. As promised, I went to the craft store and purchased silk flowers and a complementary vase. It was easy to assemble the arrangement, and I presented it to Billy the next day. He was pleased with the selection. Earlier in the morning, Billy prepared a little note to enclose with the flowers but asked if I would please rewrite it for him. He was still weak from the transplant and felt his handwriting was a bit too shaky. There was nothing elaborate about the note, simply straight from the heart, yet reading it brought tears to my eyes. My son, so stricken with pain and with barely the strength to hold a pen, somehow managed to put his own turmoil aside to cheer another.

> Dear Lori,
>
> I am sorry we have not had a chance to meet. I heard all about you and what you are going through. Most of the treatments, surgeries and infections were terrible for me, so I can't imagine what you are going through. I want you to know there are a lot of people pulling for you and I will keep you in my prayers. I hope you have a quick recovery and get well soon.
>
> > Fondly,
> > Bill Rainey

The flowers were very well received by Lori's family; her mother was touched by his gesture and sent a lovely thank-you note. I was never more proud to be Billy's mom, knowing his small act of kindness was not only treasured by another, but his heart was filled with the joy of giving; it was he who was touched by their heartfelt gratitude. "It was in giving that he received." Sad to say, Lori was unable to overcome the complications of the infection and was gently carried into the loving arms of our Lord just a few days later. I accompanied Billy to Lori's funeral. This was something he felt he had to do. He needed closure. It was an extremely hard act for me to pull off. As a mother, I did not know what to do or say to the grieving parents. I also did not feel comfortable when they told my son to hang in there, how lucky he was to be doing so well, and to continue with his remarkable recovery. I almost felt as though we shouldn't have been there. Lori did not make it, and we did. Was it fair? Did her parents think it was fair that their daughter didn't make it and my son did? So many crazy thoughts were racing through my mind. I just kept my dark glasses on and held my tissues as a safety net. Billy was his usual quiet self. He had a chance to speak with many of the nurses who were able to attend, as well as Dr. Folley, but he wasn't able to spend much time with Lori's parents in the reception area. There was a large crowd. He seemed a bit disappointed for some reason. He told me that he had something he wanted to tell Lori's mom, but he did not share that information with me.

By day thirty-five, Billy began to regain some of his appetite and strength. He was keeping fluids down, and his counts were beginning to rise. He was even beginning to regain some of his weight. Ryan would still come daily and take his counts and run the Kytril and Decadron, which made a big difference in controlling the nausea issue. We also found soothing foods for Billy to digest. He especially liked pastina, a tiny semolina pasta eaten with either chicken broth or butter. As far as calories, Billy was still getting the TPN through the PICC line every night. It was the doctor's goal to decrease the TPN and the medications slowly and get Billy back to eating healthy meals, maybe in smaller portions, and then healthy snacks in between. Around forty-one days post transfusion, Billy was to take the TPN every other day to run over a period of ten hours rather than twelve. Dr. Folley said Billy's counts were right on schedule and everything looked good. Everyone was so pleased with Billy's progress. When he went down into Dr. Berber's office, all the staff was so pleased to see him. He was showered with hugs and kisses. They couldn't get over how good he looked. It was wonderful to see everyone's expression of delight and surprise of how well Billy had overcome the bone marrow transplant. I was glad to see him smile and be the center of positive attention.

On September 24, 1998, Billy had an appointment with Dr. Berber. His weight had improved, and his counts were perfect.

It was time to prepare for the next phase of P6 protocol, the radiation. We were advised that a PET scan and a CT scan had to be done, and possibly an MRI. We would need a referral and authorization for the PET scan, and that would have to be done at a different hospital because our hospital did not have the equipment. Dr. Berber's secretary was coordinating the dates and times of these tests for me, as well as contacting the insurance company for authorization. She was a wonderful asset in Dr. Berber's office. She had a wonderful attitude and was a pleasure to be around.

There was nothing more Billy or I could do but pray and wait. The both of us crammed the next few days full with activities. Mine were all work related, and Billy tried to have some fun. He started out at the stone yard the next morning, until he started to experience shoulder pain. When he picked me up from work, I could tell by his eyes that something was wrong. He had a mellowness about him while trying to mask the pain with upbeat conversation.

When we pulled into the driveway and saw Nicole's car, Billy's mood improved. It pleased him to have his siblings home together for dinner. Something as simple as dinner with the family meant more to him than anything. He was happy to share every minute he could with them. Later that evening he rented a movie for us to watch.

At three in the morning, I was awakened by the sounds of Billy vomiting. Knowing he was rather self-conscious during these bouts of vomiting, I waited for a pause in his heaves before I knocked on the bathroom door. Billy opened the door slowly and allowed me to apply a cool washcloth to his face. There was a momentary lull in his involuntary stomach spasms, and I held him in my arms.

As I felt his forehead, I immediately knew he had a fever. The exact temperature was yet to be determined. I told Billy I needed to take his temperature because he was burning up. The thermometer revealed a temperature of 101.8 degrees. I called the hospital, and the doctor on call told me to bring him directly to the BMT unit. Maryann and Dennis were his nurses on duty, and they assisted him immediately, drawing labs and cultures. Billy was given IV fluids, Tylenol, and Ativan. Finally, around six in the morning, Billy's temperature was normal, and he had fallen asleep.

At ten o'clock, someone from transportation arrived for Billy and brought him to radiology for a chest X-ray. By that time, Billy's temperature had risen to one hundred, and they found bacteria in his urine. His hemoglobin dropped to 8.9, so they ordered an ultrasound, X-ray, and CT scan. They wanted to cover all their bases. The X-ray was inconclusive, but the ultrasound showed moderate exocrine pancreatic insufficiency. The CT scan report took several days to get read and then put into the computer, but when his cultures finally came back, they were positive for bacteria traveling through his blood stream. His temperature began to rise again throughout the night. Due to the bacteria, the urologist felt it necessary to replace the stents, and just that quickly, Billy was taken to the OR.

Prior to the procedure, the anesthesiologist ran a separate IV line for safety as well. Billy's counts were low again; therefore, he was given a unit of platelets during the surgery. The urologist personally went into the family waiting room and reported to me that the stent replacement went well. He said the stents were pretty clogged, which was from the infection. At the time, they weren't sure whether the infection began in the stents or in the port. They were hoping it was the stents, but they were still waiting for the cultures to be identified. Drs. Folley and Berber also hoped the infection started in the stents and not in the port. They told us this could potentially be a very difficult infection to treat and possibly an infection no doctor likes to see. They continued to keep a close eye on the infection and adjusted the antibiotics accordingly.

More cultures came back after the stents were removed, and they were positive for bacteria in the port traveling through his blood stream. The surgeon and the team of doctors felt it was necessary for Billy's health to remove the port, and Dr. Berber assured Billy she would personally perform the surgery. Once again, Billy looked at me with his dark brown eyes, questioning for approval. "What should I do, Mom?"

"Billy, you need to get rid of any infection traveling through your body, especially in your blood stream. You just had a transplant. You are so weak now."

"Okay, okay. I know. Yeah. Yeah. I know."

"So, we're doing this?" asked Dr. Berber. "Good. Let's set it up."

Everything was scheduled for the following day, the first thing in the morning. After a rough night of tossing and turning, Billy was up and ready when transportation arrived in his room with their wobbling, squeaky cart at seven forty-five in the morning. Typical for hospitals, though, the operation didn't start on time. Luckily, I was able to sit with Billy in the pre-op waiting room. Once they called for him, the operation itself didn't take long. Billy was back in his room by eleven thirty, wide awake and hungry. He wanted a soft pretzel and sugar wafers, and when his lunch came at twelve thirty, he ate his ham and cheese sandwich and drank his Coke. I was amazed at his appetite and happy that he was able to keep it down.

Billy slept most of the afternoon, after watching a movie, of course. And then Dr. Felix came into the room with a dark cloud. She informed us that there was a second bug found in the cultures from surgery. The bug was identified as Staphylococcus epidermi, and it would be treated with the same medication, vancomycin, as the other infection. The surgeon visited Billy's room after the dinner trays were served, and she told Billy that she took many, many cultures in the operating room. Someone from the surgical team was to visit him daily and observe the wound and change the dressing. The dressing and the stitches were removed after forty-eight hours. Another line was put in after the cultures were negative for forty-eight hours.

Dr. Michaels asked if we had made arrangements for Billy's PET scan at the University of Pennsylvania Hospital. Once again, I reminded her of the letter of necessity we needed from her. We had been waiting for her to write the letter for the insurance company to approve the scan, as Blue Cross and Blue Shield did not approve them too easily, in fact quite rarely. If we opted to pay for the test without insurance, the hospital would have given us a discount rate of $327.80 at the time of the test and three subsequent monthly payments of $327.80. We hoped our doctor's letter was sufficient for insurance approval, as we were told the PET scan was much more advanced than the CT scan or the MRI, and it gave the doctors a better look at the tumor's response to therapy. The doctors wanted a better look inside Billy's abdomen before he started with the next stage of therapy, which was radiation.

On October 2, 1998, the cultures still showed one positive and one negative. Billy's urine was a little cloudy, and the doctors were encouraging him to drink more liquids, especially water. Later that afternoon, we were graced with another visit from Dr. Michaels and a colleague, with orders for an MRI scheduled for the following Monday. She announced that a preliminary CT scan report showed positive lymph nodes and nodules on the right lung base. But the two nodules from the previous CT scan were gone. The MRI should show us more detail of what was going on. As the two doctors left, the surgical resident went in and removed the packing and redressed the wound site for Billy.

Dr. Felix was next to enter Billy's room and explained to us in a much more sensitive manner the results of the CT scan. She said the three lung nodules seen on the April CT study were no longer visualized, but two new subcentimeter nodules were seen at the right base. She would bring me my copy of the scan in

the morning. Dr. Felix also told us that two months post transplant was sometimes a little too early for a CT scan, and three
months would be more conclusive, and the MRI would show us
a little more. She also informed us that Dr. Michaels was working on a letter for the PET scan. We were not sure if that was a
good thing or not, especially after the results of the CT scan. We
would have to just wait. It was out of our hands now.

For the next three days, Billy began to show signs of a sore
throat and a cough. He was still on the vancomycin two times
daily, and he was eating well, but his temperature was lingering
around one hundred degrees. During these three days, Billy saw
a few associates but had not been visited by his primary oncologist, Dr. Michaels, at all. He had called her office several times
and was treated well by her staff. He had a great rapport with
them. Dr. Michaels even spoke to Billy on the phone and said
she would not be in on certain days but definitely others, but she
still never visited him on rounds. Every time he called her office,
he was forwarded to an associate. This was beginning to become
a habit, and Billy was getting frustrated. By now, he wanted to
know when he was scheduled for the MRI, when he was getting a
copy of the CT report, and when he was getting discharged from
the hospital. There were several questions he wanted answers to,
and she wasn't responding to him.

On the other hand, Billy was very fond of his team of physicians in the BMT unit and asked if they could be his primary
treating physicians, replacing Dr. Michaels. When he requested
something or needed emergency care and he called on them, they
always went above and beyond to care for his needs. Billy wanted
a doctor like that to progress him through the remaining phases
of P6. He wanted someone with whom he could trust and have
confidence, one who could answer his questions frankly and not
put him off to another associate.

After pondering over his situation with Dr. Michaels, Billy
visited with Dr. Folley and shared his dilemma with him. He

asked Dr. Folley if he could be his primary oncologist. Dr. Folley was diplomatic. He advised Billy not to switch doctors in the middle of treatment. He said Billy's oncologist was very good and highly recognized within her field of medicine. He further admitted that she was very possessive of her patients, but at the same time, she was quite knowledgeable of Billy's particular case. He wasn't so familiar with the P6 protocol, per se. He told Billy to think about it, to talk to Dr. Michaels about it, to be honest with her and let her know how he felt, and maybe she would bend a bit and make herself more available to him. Of course, this was not what Billy wanted to hear, but he said he would try, and try he did. He persevered with the good ol' Dr. Michaels for the remaining hospital stay, as there was not much he could do from the inside. At that time, he had to concentrate on getting well enough to go home.

Another week went by, and there was rumor that Billy could be discharged. Then we heard he could possibly get a new PICC line if his cultures remained negative for forty-eight hours. His doctor then told him they wouldn't be able to get the line in that day and he would have to stay overnight for the PICC line. There were promises of getting him in the OR the first thing in the morning, blah, blah, blah. We had heard it all so many times before. Well, believe it or not, at three o'clock in the afternoon, mysteriously, an operating room opened up. The doctor in CVIR (cardiovascular interventional radiology) was available, and Billy was hurriedly prepped and admitted to the operating room for a new port.

Once again, I was left pacing the family waiting room floor. After saying my prayers in a whispering chant, I would resort to counting the stains on the uneven, green cushions of the sofas and chairs and then start with the number of tile blocks on the floor. When my legs needed a break, I would assume a resting position against the windowsill with a magazine and flip through the pages blindly. My notebook was up to date, and there wasn't any new information to record until the surgeon came out to hopefully announce all was well. I would continue to pace until I caught a glimpse of the surgeon, and until then, none of us was ready to hear anything other than that. Fortunately, Billy was out of surgery around six o'clock in the evening, and the good doctor reported everything was fine. The surgery went well, and after a few hours, the nurses ran the vancomycin and IV fluids, and we were homeward bound.

Our next phase of this protocol was radiation therapy. While Billy had a few weeks of fairly good health and did not have to undergo any other treatments, Kevin's Uncle John had invited the boys to join him on a fishing excursion in the Florida Keys. Kevin's dad and brother also accompanied them on the trip. It was one of the most exhilarating vacations Billy had ever experienced. While they were out on the fishing vessel, Billy caught something quite large on his line, which happened to be a sailfish weighing over two-hundred pounds. It was the largest sailfish caught that entire weekend at the Sailfish Marina. The crew and Billy together struggled to get the fish aboard. He was proud as could be. I heard it in his voice when he called on the phone to announce his catch, and the glisten was still in his eyes when he returned home four days later.

Radiation Therapy

Once the port was in and the CT scan, MRI, and PET scan reports were all forwarded to Dr. Michaels, she had her nursing assistant, Diane, schedule an appointment for us to meet and discuss our next phase of therapy. The MRI and both the PET and CT scans revealed a tumor on the right pericardial region. Dr. Michaels felt it was appropriate to begin the radiation phase of therapy, but she wanted us to first meet with the radiation oncologist, Dr. Anton. Accordingly, we met with Dr. Anton, and upon our first meeting, she appeared to be quite thorough. She reviewed all of Billy's medical records, and it was apparent she knew what areas of the abdomen she was concentrating on and what organs she had to protect. Billy was impressed at her professionalism and her soft-spoken conversation, complete eye contact, and what appeared to be honest answers. She had Billy's history at her fingertips, thus eliminating the need to question him repeatedly about his past surgical experiences and his chemotherapy history. Dr. Anton was also familiar with Dr. Kushner's P6 protocol, which was another plus in her favor.

We toured the radiation facility with Dr. Anton, and it appeared her team was thorough in their preparation to radiation treatment. First and foremost, parameters of the areas to be treated with radiation were taken, which consisted of small pin dots (Billy called them his tattoos). Then the doctor discussed with us the simulation process of how they would first make a mold of Billy's trunk to keep him still and to ensure that each session he would remain in the same position for radiation. There were so many precautions. Before Billy would begin any radiation treatment, Dr. Anton wanted to make a few telephone calls, one to Dr. Michaels, making sure she had all of Billy's current blood counts, one to Billy's urologist regarding his stents during radiation, and most importantly, one to the radiation department at Sloan-Kettering regarding the doses.

Dr. Anton was up front with us regarding the side effects of the radiation. She said it would be severe for Billy, as he would be receiving very high doses of radiation. He would possibly experience abdominal cramping, nausea, vomiting, diarrhea, extreme tiredness, his bowels may get swollen, malnutrition may be incurred during radiation therapy, there could be scarring of the lungs, and there was a higher risk of heart disease. Of course, they would be administering appropriate medication to help with the nausea and vomiting. The kidneys would be blocked partially from the radiation, the liver would also be partially blocked from the radiation, and the stomach was also to be blocked from the radiation. There was a small portion of the heart that was to receive small doses of radiation and a small portion of the lung to receive radiation. The other organs not involved with the tumor were to be blocked from the radiation.

The radiation oncologists at Memorial Sloan-Kettering responded to Dr. Anton and advised that the entire abdomen was to be irradiated for two weeks at maximum doses, and then the individual organs and lymph nodes involved would be irradiated the next four weeks.

Dr. Anton was compassionate and sympathized with Billy's apprehension toward the radiation. She even called him at home and gave him a few suggestions before she started the radiation. She told him to avoid large meals and to eat small portions more frequently. She went over his medications and said Dr. Michaels agreed to write new prescriptions for Marinol and for him to keep a record of his Decadron use (how much, how often). He told her he was not looking forward to the nausea and vomiting again, and she said she was going to prescribe Ativan, Kytril, and Decadron at night. It seemed they worked better together. She told Billy they would take a full abdominal X-ray or CT scan so they could see the entire field to be irradiated. She said their files were not that large for the port simulation, and she wanted to be precise with the organ blocks, especially the liver. The liver cannot take the radiation. She said they would finish the simulation in two more days. Billy was comfortable enough to go back himself the next day to have the liver block redone, as the first one was too large. Once the molds were completed, we were ready to begin treatment.

November 16, 1998, Billy received his first radiation treatment. We had to be there by seven o'clock in the morning. Dr. Anton reviewed the X-rays with us and revealed where the disease was on the diaphragm. Billy's second treatment was scheduled for the afternoon. By the time we got home, he was really tired and surprisingly, he slept through the night.

In the morning, we went over our game plan for the remaining weeks of treatment. Billy said he wanted to go by himself for his treatments for as long as he could. He said he would stay the day. They gave him lunch, and he was able to rest between treatment sessions. He said it was easier than having two of us sit there. Besides, he had fun with the nurses, and if he wanted to sleep, he could sleep; the lounge chairs were comfortable. He promised that if it was too much for him, he would call me and I would take him home. He said this way I could go to work a few hours or even get in a full day. I knew he wanted some independence, and I knew he was thinking of me, so I agreed and said we would play it by ear.

The following week, Billy went to the hospital alone for his treatments. The nurses were all good to him. He ordered turkey and cheese sandwiches for lunch and talked about his fishing trip. The nurses and aides were all anxious to see his pictures, and he was proud to share his memories of the trip with them. I would ask him what they did at therapy, and he said the radiation techs did more drawing on his abdomen the second day of treatment. He said they were still making small adjustments with the lead blocks. He went home exhausted, and he slept through the night. His appetite hadn't yet improved, so we started the TPN three times a week. Billy's home nurse continued to draw his labs, but on radiation days, he would go to the center and have them drawn there. Everyone was so accommodating for Billy.

After a few days of radiation therapy, Billy was showing signs of fatigue, but he was determined to fight it. One night he took his little brother Sean to the movies to see one of his favorite actors, Adam Sandler, in his new movie, *The Waterboy*. A few days later, he embarked on another project when his pictures from his fishing trip arrived; he was determined to stay up until he completed the photo album.

Radiation treatment was continuing, and the holiday season was fast approaching. On good days, Billy and I would try to do some shopping. One particular day we went to the mall, stopping for short breaks in between. We were able to get a few things done. Once we returned home, he took a long nap in the afternoon while I baked biscotti for the nurses. Billy enjoyed bringing goodies in for the nurses as much as they enjoyed receiving them. They were always so grateful, but I was the most grateful one. I'll never be able to express my gratitude for the tender loving care they gave my son.

Billy was anxious to finally show the nurses and techs his pictures. Everyone was amazed at the size of the sailfish he caught and how wonderful he looked on his trip. His enthusiasm and energy from his trip spilled over into the photo album, and his eyes lit up every time he showed it to someone. I am so indebted to Kevin and his Uncle John for inviting Billy on that trip. They'll never know how much it meant to him.

We were so happy to have spent Thanksgiving at home that year. This was a special treat, as the last year we spent Thanksgiving in the hospital. My brother Joseph enjoyed dinner with us, and my sister and her children went for dessert. My ex-brother-in-law Alan also stopped by, and my Billy was beaming when he saw him. He was touched that Alan thought enough to make the special trip to see him.

Slowly, Billy's platelets were dropping. His white counts were dropping as well. We had to start up with the Neupogen injections for four days. His counts were low, and he continued to need platelets. We had to stop radiation for one and a half weeks. We had to start the Neupogen again, this time for five more days. Billy continued to go to the Bodine Center for platelets, and his counts finally began to come back. On December 18, 1998, we had to end radiation altogether. Our radiologist called Dr. Kushner at Sloan-Kettering, who was in agreement to discontinue the treatment. Billy had had enough. His system could not tolerate another ounce of radiation. He was dehydrated and in immediate need of blood products and IV fluids.

We tried several times to meet with Dr. Michaels and get Billy's counts. We felt as though we were being put off. She would either ask us to call her later, or we would get a voice mail. After several days of playing phone tag, Billy decided this was the last time he was playing this game with her. He decided to make an appointment with Dr. Brown, the department head oncologist at

Jefferson. We were finally seen a few days before Christmas, and he was very gentle, likable, and he acknowledged Billy's needs. He was familiar with Billy's chart and had us continue with the Neupogen injections and blood products, as Billy's platelets were still very low.

On New Year's Eve day, we had to go to the hospital, and once again, Billy needed two units of platelets. When the infusion was complete, Billy was seen by the urologist, who suggested a follow-up appointment for his pre-admission testing. Due to the high amounts of radiation, Billy needed the stents replaced again. Surgery for the stent-replacement went smoothly and without any complications. Therefore, Billy was able to go home once he completed the IV fluids. A few days after the surgery, Billy went to the hospital for blood products, but he was once again dehydrated, and they admitted him and immediately started to run IV fluids and two units of blood and two units of platelets. Dr. Folley informed us he had just returned from a conference at Sloan-Kettering, where he had an opportunity to speak with the doctors about Billy's counts. The New York doctors advised Dr. Folley that most of their patients needed a boost of their stem cells after a transplant if they showed no signs of recovery on their own. It was their opinion that Billy probably would not show signs of recovery on his own, and he would be receiving repeated transfusions until then.

Once admitted, Dr. Folley started Billy on IV fluids immediately. He administered Ativan and Benedryl to help him sleep, and started the Neupogen injections again. The urine cultures were negative for blood but positive for an infection. The cultures were sent to pathology. In the interim, he was started on antibiotics. Dr. Folley assured Billy that he would be able to go home a day or two after the transfusion and that he shouldn't experience too many adverse reactions since he would not be receiving chemotherapy with the stem cell boost. There was a possibility, however, that he would experience some nausea from the DSM preservative.

Stem Cell Transfusion Boost

January 11, 1999, Billy was given pre-medications consisting of one hundred milligrams of Benedryl and four milligrams of Ativan and Tylenol. The room was prepped, the special freezer unit containing the stem cells was rolled in, and the infusion began. Donned in my yellow gown and mask, I stood by Billy, ready to help in any way I could. Once the cells came out of the freezer unit, their identification numbers were checked and verified. They were placed in the defroster for just a short time then immediately infused through the port. The cells had to be infused while still frozen, and I can only imagine how it felt going through Billy's veins. He felt sick after the initial bag was infused. Then he started with the hiccups. After a brief rest, they began the second bag and the third. Then Billy experienced pain in his ear, along with popping. The technician, Dennis, switched IV lines from the white to the red while I ran to get cotton for his ears. The infusion continued, and Billy was given another two milligrams of Ativan before they started infusing the sixth bag into his veins. Once everyone finished their part in the infusion,

Billy was shivering from the ice-cold stem cells flowing through his bloodstream, so we wrapped him in heated blankets and kept him warm. When he felt he could tolerate something to eat, I gave him a soft pretzel and ginger ale. Then he fell fast asleep.

Billy woke up the next morning complaining of neck pain and a headache. He said he had been getting infrequent headaches, which was unusual, as Billy rarely suffered from them. I questioned the nurses if the headaches had any significance to the infusion. They were not certain but assured me they would call the doctor and advise him. Dennis suggested the possibility of the PICC line slipping out of place, and Dr. Folley agreed to order a chest X-ray. Sure enough, the PICC line had in fact moved up into Billy's neck toward his head. Thank goodness Dennis spoke up about the chest X-ray. The nurses on staff were surprised, as was the resident who said he had never seen a PICC line move up before. Consequently, the nurses had to run a separate IV line for Billy's meds until the PICC line was changed. An appointment was made with Cardiovascular interventional radiology to have his line changed in the morning. In the meantime, Dennis had some difficulty starting an IV in Billy's left arm, so Denise stepped in, and she was successful. Billy asked me to bring chicken noodle soup for dinner. That was about all he was able to tolerate along with his ginger ale. By eight thirty in the evening, he was ready for his Ativan and Benedryl cocktail. At nine thirty I headed for home after he coaxed me into giving him leg and back massages. Billy had been experiencing leg cramps, which were a new symptom that the doctors were going to look into.

Before Billy could go to CVIR in the morning, he needed more blood products. His platelets were low and needed to be infused. This setback caused him to lose his time slot in the morning, and he was kept waiting all day for the next opening in their schedule. I ran into the office for a few hours and waited for Billy's call. He did call a few times to tell me he was bored.

He was sitting around in his room in anticipation and was a bit frustrated that he had missed his time slot. He wanted to get the new line in so he could go home, so I left work a little early to wait with Billy. By the time I arrived, he was hungry, so I headed for the cafeteria. When I stepped onto the elevator, there was Dr. Folley. He expressed his delight that Billy was going home after the CVIR procedure. He said maybe we would be home in time for the snowstorm. He knew how much Billy loved the snow. I told him Billy had been waiting all day for CVIR and he had missed his slot because of an infusion in the morning. The good doctor said he would see what he could do for us, and by the time Billy finished eating, CVIR called, and the new line was put in.

After the procedure, Billy needed red blood (PAC) cells. While the second bag of red blood product was being infused, Billy complained of terrible pain in his head. He asked me to massage his temples. The pain intensified, so I called his nurse. Dennis went in, and he immediately called the doctor. They stopped the blood temporarily and called Dr. Folley at home. When Dennis flushed Billy's line, he applied a lot of pressure, and then Billy's ears popped. We (Dennis and I) knew at that point it was definitely the new line. The resident didn't think so, but she had Dennis stop the fluids and flush the line again. Sure enough, Billy had ear and head pain again. By eight o'clock, Billy went for another chest X-ray, which showed that the new line had moved up. Unfortunately, Billy was unable to go home as planned, and I could see the disappointment in his eyes when I left for home around ten o'clock. It broke my heart to leave, but it was getting late, and I had to get home for the boys. I told him I would be there for his procedure in the morning. Billy was scheduled once more for this PICC line to be surgically repaired or another replacement line put in.

Again, in the morning, Billy needed a platelet infusion. Someone lost his chest X-ray from the night prior, and CVIR techs didn't believe his line moved a second time. They subjected Billy to yet another chest X-ray, which did confirm their line had moved…again. When I called Billy to see what time his procedure was scheduled, he told me not to hurry because he was bumped again because of the platelets and now another chest X-ray. He told me I might as well go to the office for a few hours and said he would call me when they were ready for him. When CVIR called for him, Billy requested sedation for the line replacement and wanted me there. He called me, but at the time, I needed to get a project out that I had started, and I wasn't finished. I was surprised they called for him so early and was torn that I could not be there. I called his dad, and he was able to go to the hospital until I could finish my work.

The procedure went well, and Billy and his dad were able to get home before me. Billy felt fine but was hungry. I promised him whatever he wanted for dinner, and Billy requested white pizza. He was glad to be home. I was glad he was home too. We all were. The family dynamics were different without Billy, and when we were all around the dinner table, you could just feel the energy between the boys. We were all bonded as one. We truly were family. Of course, the typical bantering between siblings continued, but in a fun way, and we all had a good laugh now and then. Sometimes we laughed just for the sake of laughing. These are the memories we hold dear to our hearts—the nonsense and the giggles, the looks and the jokes between themselves, and the hand signals and gestures behind my back.

●

Billy took Matthew and Sean to the electronics store to inquire about an alarm system he was purchasing for his car. He was having it installed while he was in the hospital for the PICC line replacement. After driving Matthew to work, Billy coaxed me into going to the mall with him and Sean. He particularly wanted to go to Sears and look at the sixty-gallon air compressors, after which he and Sean had a ball looking at all the puppies in the pet store. I suppose it was safe to say we all fell in love with the face on a cocker spaniel. I never realized how expensive they were. We stopped for a hot beverage and headed home. It was getting late, and I still had to administer Billy's meds. He was so tired. He fell fast asleep.

Billy complained of achy joints when I ran the vancomycin at seven the following morning. I gave him Ativan two hours later, and he still had pain. I tried Tylenol and then Dilaudid, and he still complained. Ryan was scheduled to come at ten o'clock, but the weather was bad, and Ryan called around ten thirty and said he wasn't coming. I called Lori at Dr. Folley's office because Billy's pain was increasing. She told us to go to the clinic. In the meantime, I had to run to the Jersey office to get the mail out. My boss had not signed the past two days' work, and when I got there, it still wasn't done, and there was nothing I could do about it. I alerted the Philadelphia office of the status of the mail at the office and that I had to bring Billy to the hospital. It was an emergency.

Hurriedly we got into the car, I drove Billy to the hospital with butterflies in my stomach the entire ten miles. My body was shaking. It took so much strength to keep my hand steady on the wheel and my concentration on the road. I continually glanced over to Billy and tried to make conversation with him to keep him alert.

By the time we reached the hospital, his vision was blurred, and he said his hearing was diminished. The staff was aware we were coming and upon our arrival, they had a wheelchair waiting for us and brought him to an examination room. Intravenous fluids were started immediately, and Lori took his vitals and started him on a Cipro IV. She ordered a chest X-ray and admitted Billy to the BMT unit. Upon admittance, Billy's blood pressure was down to sixty, so we waited until it went up to seventy. Then we literally ran, with Lori pushing Billy in the wheelchair, to the unit. An attendant, Wayne, carried the IV fluids for us. Marianne and Ray ran to get his labs, fluids, antibiotics, etc. All the doctors on Billy's team went in to Billy's room and said he was septic. His blood pressure was dangerously low, and they had to put him on dopamine to elevate the pressure. He was in septic shock, renal failure, and sinus tachycardia. There was an entire team working on Billy.

I had to move to the back of the room and observe and pray. I had my rosary in my pocket, and my fingers were moving faster than my lips. I was reciting, "Hail Mary, full of grace..." over and over. Billy was in distress, glancing at me in a daze. Then his head would drop, and his eyes would close. I knew he was scared, and so was I.

They started Billy on a morphine drip at a continuous flow rate of 4mg per hour, and when Billy's pain did not respond, they raised the basal rate to 8mg per hour, and then they maxed the drip out at 9.9mg per hour. He continued to complain that his joint pain was severe, especially in his ankles and knees. His dopamine started at four then increased to eight, and whenever we would stop the fluids for blood work or cultures, his pressure would drop. A specialist from infectious disease was called in to see Billy, asking him questions and observing his signs to assess the severity of the infection. After listening to his lungs and heart, she conferred with the resident, who felt the infection was coming from his PICC line, and decided to abort all medications through the PICC line as a precaution until the infection was identified. They felt a femoral line would be the best solution. Two nurses assisted the resident putting in a femoral line in Billy's groin. Billy insisted he did not want it there, but the doctors explained that it was a life-threatening situation.

It was crucial to have the medications run through a line and because there were too many fluids and antibiotics running; they could not use a simple IV line. Billy looked at me his eyes pleading for an answer I could not give. At that moment, I was at a total loss for words. I asked the doctors if there were any other options. I thought there had to be alternatives, something less invasive for my son. The doctors said there were only two options: either the femoral line in his neck or the femoral line in his groin. This was a decision my son had to make on his own. It was his body, and he was the one who had to choose where he would best tolerate an invasive tube. The doctor continued to tell Billy it was his choice. I could see the disappointment in Billy's eyes, and I could only imagine how he felt. Some choice. Reluctantly, Billy opted for his groin.

After the ordeal of the femoral line being placed, Billy was administered vancomycin, dopamine, Cipro, acyclovir, and Diflucan, along with PSS fluids, Kytril, Ativan, and morphine. The lab technicians continued to draw labs throughout the night, monitoring his progress. Shortly after Billy finished his breakfast, his nurse came in and announced that yet another problem arose. Billy was not putting out enough urine, so they had to insert a Foley catheter. They had his IV fluids up to two hundred, and his output gradually increased. Then he began to void in excess, and they had to lower his fluid intake. Needless to say, we were up all night making adjustments to Billy's medications and fluids as the lab results came back. Luckily, the chest X-ray and that of his belly were both fine, but the venous gases they drew showed his counts to be out of whack, and they had to run sodium bicarbonate; his Ph levels were too low; magnesium was low; his potassium was low. Billy was retaining fluid in his joints and wasn't able to get much sleep, maybe little cat naps, ten to fifteen minutes at a time. His blood pressure, however, did become stable with the dopamine; unfortunately, it continued to drop every time we stopped the fluids to run labs. We kept Billy on oxygen all night as well. His oxygen levels continued to drop without it, and his heart rate was still high. I sat by his bed all night, listening to pumps beeping and the oxygen valve opening and closing with each breath Billy took.

I was afraid to walk away. I prayed all these tubes and pumps would soon be gone. My son's every limb was poked and prodded for either medicine injections or lab draws, and my heart sank when I counted every stitch and physical scar he had accumulated during this ordeal. I was having a hard time praying. There were so many thoughts racing through my mind. All I could do was ask God to please free my son of this burden. I begged for a miracle. My son needed healing, his body had been beaten down, and I saw discouragement in his face for the first time. It was too much for me to bear to see my son suffer. My faith was being tested. How could I just let go and let God? Sure, it was easy for someone else to tell me to let go and let God, but how could I trust now? My prayers weren't being answered; rather than seeing progress in my son's condition, all I saw were more roadblocks and detours. I was hanging on by a thread, but I had to keep strong for Billy. Watching him lie helplessly in a hospital bed with oxygen pumps and intravenous tubing hanging from a pole above his bed was all too surreal. I had nothing to give my son but my love and my faith. I had to believe God would not desert me now.

Billy made it through the night. It was a little rough on all of us, but he made it. He was still in a lot of pain, especially his ankles and knees. He asked for Benedryl all night, but the nurse could only give him twenty-five milligrams in combination with the morphine. The doctors felt it would bring his blood pressure down, so they gave him Ativan. The nurses started his morphine at four milligrams, and then it went to six milligrams and then eight milligrams. Dan, one of Billy's favorite nursing assistants, brought in the PCA pump for Billy, and once it was hooked up, a nurse gave him a bolus of morphine, which immediately triggered a sharp shooting pain throughout his joints. Fifteen minutes later, when Billy pushed the button himself on the pump, he experienced the same shooting sensation throughout his body. I saw him grimace, and I told the resident and nurse. They stopped the morphine pushes and lowered the basal rate of the morphine as well. When the resident was more comfortable with Billy's blood pressure, he lowered the dopamine.

Maribeth was Billy's nurse in the morning; and Dennis and Denise, his night-shift nurses, went to visit him. They were all very surprised to see him back in the unit so soon and quite concerned at how sick he was. While the nurses were still there, the infectious disease doctor went in Billy's room and reported to us the culture from his port was positive for gram-negative infection. She said gram negative was the worse type of infection in the blood stream and the way to treat this was to get him started on a heavy-duty antibiotic specific for that bacteria. We were all thankful he was not neutropenic. Thank God, we started him back on the Neupogen. Billy's nurses told him they had everything under control. They would take care of him, and he knew they would. He trusted them. He knew they truly cared. I thanked them as they left his room and gave them each a gentle hug.

The cardiopulmonary resident and attending physician evaluated Billy; they were concerned about his heart rate and oxygen levels and told him to keep his oxygen on until told otherwise. Afterward, Dr. Folley and the BMT unit team went in to see Billy. They appeared to be pleased with the gradual improvement in his pain level from the previous night. They were also very happy to see that the most recent ultrasound report confirmed his kidneys and bladder were functioning within normal limits. There was an increase in swelling in Billy's knees, so Dr. Folley recommended a rheumatologist evaluate the joint pain, and he said he would be there shortly. Billy waited a while, but no one ever showed up. He was a bit tired, but he needed blood and platelets. Maribeth was able to give him fifty milligrams of Benedryl until the blood products arrived. After Billy received his blood products, he was comfortable and able to rest in bed. I decided to run home, get a bath, and get clean clothes for Billy and myself.

By the time I returned to the hospital, Maribeth had Billy's blood pressure stabilized and he was off the dopamine. Cardiopulmonary ordered another chest X-ray and cortisone every eight hours for two days to help stabilize Billy's respiratory rate. The latest CBC showed Billy's levels were all within normal limits. Our one drawback that day was Billy's fever. It spiked to 102. Tylenol brought it down slightly, but only temporarily. He was still on antibiotics to help with his many types of infections. The specific bacteria had not yet been determined.

Due to the fever spikes and medications, Billy's mouth had been dry, and he had been drinking a lot of juice and water. His lips were dry and chapped, and something had been causing him to itch. I had been sponging his mouth to keep it moist and applying Chapstick to his lips, and we tried Atarax for the itching, but that didn't help much. Billy then felt like snacking on something, so I ran to the vending machine and purchased pretzels and chips. Later in the evening, he asked if they had donuts at the nursing station. When I inquired, Christy, a nurse on duty at the time, was able to find him some coffee cake. Billy was thrilled. That was his favorite. I made him hot chocolate, and he drank that with his cake, a little bit at a time, in between cat-naps. Around midnight he finally fell asleep, as did I. The nurse went in a few times to get his vitals, but he was able to return to a deep sleep. Early in the morning, Christy woke Billy up. He had broken into a sweat. The fever finally broke, but his respiratory rate kept dropping while he was sleeping. The nurse wanted him to breath through his nose to see if he could get his rate up. She stayed up with him for about an hour, after which time he wanted pretzels and soda. Then he fell back to sleep for another hour.

Billy was able to eat a full breakfast in the morning, and the resident lowered his morphine basal rate to 2.2. Billy was still sleepy, and his response time was delayed. When Ray, his day nurse, came on duty, he administered Billy's Ativan and increased his oxygen rate. Billy's nose, being dry all night and continuing so in the morning, which caused him to scratch and rub it frequently, began to bleed. Ray then ordered a nasal spray to keep his nasal passages moist, and he removed the nose tube oxygen syringe and replaced it with an oxygen facemask. Once Billy felt more comfortable, he was able to take a little nap before being probed and prodded at again.

When the resident went in with the team, they discussed a gram-negative bacteria that travels through the body in rods. The rheumatologist who evaluated Billy joined the doctors, and collectively, they wanted to ascertain whether the fluids in Billy's joints were indeed gram-negative rods so they could address the joint disease. Whatever the bacteria, it was still running through Billy's blood stream, and they did not want it to settle in his joints. Now I was confused, as the infectious disease doctor said it was gram negative, and now they were questioning whether it really was. When I questioned them, they explained there were several different types of bacteria and that was what they were trying to identify.

The lab was able to identify the bacteria as *Pseudomanas*, which we were told was a "nasty" bacteria. The team was still waiting for the specifics. They said, "Billy is making progress. He is not completely out of the woods, but he is recovering." Billy's platelets were low, down to fifteen, and he needed another infusion. Though his appetite was healthy, his physical body was weak. It took two men, Billy's nurse Ray and Jack—his aide—to help Billy out of bed and into the recliner so they could make his bed.

Later that day when Kevin visited Billy, he asked Kevin to bring him a Chick-Fil-A sandwich and waffle fries, after which he ate an apple donut, peaches, and Jell-O. The nursing staff couldn't believe Billy's appetite. The BMT team agreed this was the first admission not related to nausea and vomiting. Billy did, however, continue to need oxygen. The pulmonologist went in to speak with Billy, stressing the importance of mobility and decreasing pain medications, coughing and using the spirom-eter. He was concerned with the amount of fluid Billy had been retaining. He also ordered another chest X-ray and monitored Billy's progress closely. He added Lasix to Billy's IV medications, and by that evening, when Maribeth was on duty, Billy had put out fourteen hundred ccs of fluid. They were glad to see his kid-neys were working.

During the night, Billy had a tickle in his throat that devel-oped into a coughing fit lasting twenty minutes and continuing intermittently throughout the night. During his coughing spells, he would remove the oxygen, and his SP02 rate would drop to sixty-nine. It was evident he had to keep the oxygen on. If it had slipped off, I had to be sure to get it back on. We were told it was crucial for Billy to sit up and use the spirometer and to cough as much as possible, because his next twenty-four hours were cru-cial to avoid intubation or bronchoscopy. If questionable, Billy would have been subjected to more accurate tests. Billy was able to sit upright, and he used the spirometer as frequently as possi-ble, while at the same time keeping his oxygen mask on as much as possible. Billy was gradually weaned off his pain medicine, and eventually his oxygen was reduced to 20 percent on the nasal can-ula overnight. The doctor's goal was to keep him at ninety-three with the nasal canula and then wean him off the oxygen slowly.

The next day was nonstop for Billy. The resident removed the femoral line, as they can be a great source of infection. Then Billy went to CVIR for another PICC line in his right arm. A new antibiotic regimen was started. Urology went in and drew fluids. Billy needed two units of platelets and one unit of red blood then was poked and prodded by a new resident. Billy just wanted to sleep and begged for his Ativan and Benedryl. The two nurses on duty were new, and there was no way they were going to give him his meds early. They were running around the floor, totally overwhelmed with their new task at hand, so Billy and I just sat there and waited until we saw a familiar face. Finally, when I spotted Anne Marie, I coaxed her to administer Billy's bedtime cocktail so he could sleep after his nightmarish day. Once he was settled, I told him I had to go home to the boys because his dad had to go to work. Billy wasn't happy that I was leaving, but he knew Matthew and Sean couldn't stay alone all night. I stayed with him until he fell asleep, and then I hesitantly tiptoed out of his room.

When I returned the next morning, Billy told me he had had a rough night, and I was sorry I couldn't be there for him. He did, however, look better. His blood pressure was low, but his SPO level was up to ninety-six without the oxygen. Shortly after my arrival, Billy was greeted by a parade of doctors. The infectious disease doctor went in and told Billy she wanted him to have two weeks of antibiotic therapy. The resident doctor said if Billy's cultures came back negative two consecutive days, there was a possibility he could go home. Then the rheumatologist told him there was still fluid in the knees and ankles, but it was probably residual from the infection. He ordered more X-rays and said he would review them personally. Billy then received a visit from the director of the oncology department who remarked he was glad Billy looked as good as he did and offered his open-door policy to us should we ever have a problem in the future. He said he was following Billy's progress and wanted us to know that he was there and in our corner. We found this an odd time for him to visit us, but nevertheless, he was aware of Billy's situation.

Sure enough, Billy's cultures did return with negative results for two consecutive days, and as promised, they were working on a discharge for Billy. After receiving two more units of platelets, bringing them up to eighty-thousand for the weekend, Billy was finally able to go home. The BMT team and I worked feverishly with the home health aides and JHIS to get his IV meds and supplies coordinated for his homecoming. The resident gave me instructions for administering the IV medications, and Lori and Janet said they would both be in the unit on Sunday. If Billy noticed blood in his urine, he was to go directly to the BMT unit. Lori would administer the platelets herself. Otherwise, Billy had a scheduled appointment in the clinic on Monday at one o'clock for platelets and an appointment with Dr. Folley at three o'clock.

Thankfully, the weekend was uneventful. I was able to work my part-time job Saturday evening and Sunday afternoon, while Sean assisted Billy with his three-o'clock dose of meds on Sunday. On Monday, Bill took Billy to the hospital for his one-o'clock platelet appointment, but only dropped him off at the door, and I met Billy at the clinic around two o'clock; but his platelets didn't finish running until a few minutes before his three-o'clock appointment with Dr. Folley, at which time he requested we schedule an appointment with Dr. Kushner. Dr. Folley felt we would have more detailed information concerning the progress of the treatment once we received the CT scan and the MRI reports. He assured us he would be working closely with Dr. Kushner from that point on. For the time being, Dr. Folley said he was concerned about my well-being, and he spoke on a personal note of him being in a critical situation with his own daughter and knowing how it wore on a parent. He did not elaborate on his daughter's illness, and I was sorry I didn't ask him more details. I wondered if I should have called him and asked him about his daughter, but Billy said if he wanted me to know more he would have told me, or at least elaborated. I felt Billy was full of wisdom, and I followed his lead. We both shared the feeling that Dr. Folley was so much more concerned about his patients than any other doctor we had encountered up to that point. I only hoped that one day I would be able to express our true appreciation to him. I always seemed to be at a lack for words when I saw him.

During his next few appointments, Billy felt strong enough and insisted on taking the trip to Jefferson independently for his platelet injections at nine o'clock in the morning. He would take the Speedline in to the city, and I would meet him there for lunch.

One particular appointment he spent most of the day waiting for his injections. Not happy at all, he called me at work. I told him I would be there as soon as I could. Quite concerned, I called Madeline and was told Lori forgot to write the orders, which caused the delay. I was able to leave work and stayed with Billy the remaining part of the afternoon, calmed him down, and we went home together. After that incident, the platelet injections usually ran smoothly. Billy tired very easily during that time. He had the will to do things, and he would attempt to do them but could never follow through. For example, he would get up and go to the stone yard, but an hour or two later, he would return home and take a nap. I would run home from the office to run his afternoon meds, and he would be either napping or lying down trying to nap. If I went to work during the evening, I would return home and find him fast asleep and would have to wake him for his bedtime IV meds. This continued up until the day Billy went for his MRI and CT scan, and I debated whether it was time for me to quit my part-time job. Billy told me it was not necessary, as he was just sleeping and there was nothing I could do for him while he was sleeping. I was terribly torn. I was afraid that if I quit my job he would worry that I felt there was something terribly wrong, yet if I continued to work, as my mother constantly reminded me, would I have regrets later? The decision was tearing me apart, but I had to consider Billy's mindset at the time. All I wanted to do was continue to give him hope.

On February 1, 1999, Billy and I got up early and checked in at the Main Hospital on Chestnut Street. We were then directed to go to the Walnut Street building down to the radiology department. The building itself was nice and clean and quiet. We did not have to wait very long until they called Billy to follow the technician into the back for the MRI. I remember waiting quite a while for Billy and was getting nervous. I didn't remember any of his other MRIs taking so long. Finally, Billy went back into the waiting room, and I was relieved to see him; he looked exhausted.

He sat next to me and didn't say much as he sat there. There was a long silence before I spoke.

"Billy, how was it? Are you okay? Do you feel nauseous?"

"No, I'm fine. I'm just tired. I could have fallen asleep in that tunnel if it wasn't so loud. They gave me earplugs, but it was still loud. I don't know if it was a new tech or not. Not sure if they knew what they were doing. Seems like they had to do something over again. It was getting frustrating after a while."

"Really?" And then I added a sarcastic "hmm," as if to say I wasn't surprised.

But I didn't want to get him any more frustrated. I knew how these tests made him feel confined and grated on his nerves. I wanted him to remain as calm as possible. I tried to change the subject, and we began to talk about the upcoming forecast of possible snow. That seemed to brighten Billy's eyes. We hadn't had a snowstorm in a while, and Billy was looking forward to plowing in the big truck. After about a half hour in the waiting room, Billy was called for his CT scan, which did not take long at all, and we were able to head for home. We had a follow-up appointment with Dr. Folley to discuss the test results, and I requested a copy to be sent to me as well. All we could do was wait for the results.

We met with Dr. Anton three days prior to our visit with Dr. Kushner, and she suggested we ask Dr. Kushner if we needed another PET scan. She thought maybe Billy should be checked every three months with a CT scan and MRI and possibly cut back on his TPN once Billy got to 150 to 160 pounds.

Both Billy's and my heads were spinning by the time we sat in Dr. Kushner's office. We had so many questions jotted down in my notebook, and Billy had so many thoughts racing through his mind that didn't quite make it to paper. Neither of us quite knew where to begin. Billy just looked at me when Dr. Kushner entered the room and shook our hands and asked, "Well, how are you? First off, what questions do you have for me?"

Billy began with his stomach and bowel issues and how long he had endured them. He didn't buy that they were a side effect of the radiation, because he had gone through this from the beginning. First it was a symptom of the tumor, then he was sick from the chemotherapy treatment, and then it continued even after they stopped the radiation. He did ask if the doctor thought it was a good idea to postpone the surgery for a little while until he felt a little stronger or if Dr. Kushner believed it should have been done sooner rather than later. I pulled out my notebook and listed Billy's medications for the doctor's review and left the room while he examined Billy. After the examination, I was called back into the room and listened to what Dr. Kushner proposed for Billy. He wanted Billy to have a pulmonary-function test (PFT), an audiogram, an echocardiogram, and a PET scan. He wanted the tests done at Memorial Sloan-Kettering Hospital, as he preferred his physicians administer the tests so the films and results were there for him to review personally. Dr. Kushner's assistant was assigned the task of arranging the tests all on the same day, for our traveling convenience, and she had called us with the date.

●

Toward the end of February, Billy started to lose his appetite again. I could tell something was wrong, and he was not voiding within normal amounts. When Ryan went to draw routine labs, Billy had a temperature of 99.6, and he was tachycardic. When I called the unit, Lori advised me to start one liter of fluids (PSS) daily for three days. I had one liter at home, so I was able to begin immediately. I asked Ryan if I should start with the Decadron in conjunction with the Kytril, and he said no. We started with the Ativan every two hours as needed, and the Kytril up to three times a day, if necessary. The fluids seemed to help Billy toward the late afternoon, although he had a rough night. I slept downstairs with him so I could continue with the Ativan throughout the night.

The next few nights were very rough for Billy. The emesis continued. I started the IV fluids a little earlier in the evening, and that seemed to help. Billy then began to show signs and symptoms of a head cold with nasal congestion and coughing. I had him sit in the shower with the steam. I continued with the Kytril, Ativan, and Benedryl as directed and made Jell-O, which Billy was able to eat in small portions. Billy was starting to get some relief from the nausea and vomiting by the third day of IV liquids and meds. He was able to tolerate small amounts of soup and ginger ale as well. By the afternoon, he even had the stamina to work on Anthony's pinewood derby car. He said he felt well enough for me to go to work, so I ran to my second job for a few hours in the evening. While I was there, his radiation oncologist, Dr. Anton, was shopping in my department. Surprised to see me, we talked for a long time, She was glad we were seeing Dr. Kushner, yet she was surprised he wanted a PET scan. I told her that Dr. Kushner warned us about the radiation side effects beginning three months post radiation, and that the bout of emesis Billy was experiencing might have been effects Dr. Kushner was referring to. She advised us to keep our appointment unless Billy was so sick he couldn't make the trip. I agreed with her. After my shift ended, Billy and I ran to Sean's final hockey playoff game at Hollydell. By the time we returned home, it was time to start the TPN and bedtime medications. Billy started coughing again, so I slept downstairs with him to make sure he didn't start vomiting. Both Billy and I were exhausted by the time our heads hit the pillow.

Ryan continued his routine dressing changes and labs and collected a twenty-four-hour urine sample for Dr. Kushner. Billy was still coughing and complaining of nausea. His output was still low, and his urine was concentrated. I called Dr. Felix with questions regarding Billy's most recent lab work. His hemoglobin had dropped, WBC had dropped, and his platelets had dropped. She also had his labs from that current day in front of her, which showed they had dropped even further. She advised they were alerted to his counts but he was not at the danger level yet. They were not pleased that the counts were going down, but there could be several factors, so they would keep a close eye on them. She wanted to see what Dr. Kushner had to say about the labs.

On March 2, 1999, Billy and I went to New York for the PFT (pulmonary-function test), echocardiogram, and audiogram. Billy was not feeling well when he awoke at four thirty in the morning to get ready for the trip to New York. He brought his pillow and blanket in the car and slept while I drove. When we arrived at Memorial Sloan-Kettering, I was able to get a wheelchair for him. He was much too weak to even walk. We arrived at the clinic at eight o'clock. Our appointment was scheduled for nine, but they were actually happy that we arrived a bit early. They took Billy's weight and temperature and a blood stick. No surprise, Billy had a slight fever again at 99.7. His weight had stayed the same, which we were thankful for. The nurse had instructed us where to go for each of the tests and told us to return to the pediatric day hospital (PDH) after each test.

The PFT included a blood gases test. Billy had to stop during the test, as the emesis began. The technician was patient and gentle with him and allowed me to stay in the room with Billy for the remainder of the test. When he completed the test, we returned to the PDH waiting area, where we were surprised to see the other DSRCT patient from Jefferson, Bob McCarthy. While speaking with Bob, we caught of glimpse of Dr. Kushner from afar, he acknowledged us, though he appeared to be in quite a hurry. Bob couldn't say enough nice things about Dr. Kushner, affirming he was the best doctor in the world. Bob divulged information about two other male patients he had met here in New York with the same diagnosis. He said both seemed to have had good results from the protocol, and they were both treated at Memorial Sloan-Kettering. They sang their praises of Dr. Kushner to Bob, declaring he was the best oncologist in the country. Bob also shared tidbits of information with Billy regarding his stay at the Ronald McDonald House, where he was staying during his radiation treatments. It was a nice visit for Billy. It helped him feel a little better and more optimistic about his treatments. He and Bob shared a few personal war stories about their own histories and how they had overcome some horrible aftereffects. They again exchanged phone numbers and wished each other well, hoping to meet again at Jefferson.

Bob looked good and appeared to be doing well. But he said his tumor had moved up to the thoracic area and he had to receive radiation to the neck and throat area for two weeks and after that, radiation to the abdomen for two weeks, which was also done at Sloan-Kettering. He told Billy he felt more comfortable getting his protocol treatments from Dr. Kushner. He spent a lot of time in New York, so he gave Billy his e-mail address to keep in touch and said he liked to bring his laptop with him to occupy his time while away from home. His dad was staying with him that week, though he wasn't too comfortable with the responsibility of his care. He said his mom did mostly everything for him; she was a nurse. He said his dad got nervous when he went home because he didn't like to wait in the ER if he got sick and needed to be hospitalized. Billy said we were fortunate in that respect. We had a direct line with the BMT unit, avoiding the long wait at the ER. Bob said the BMT unit never called him regarding his transplant, and I told him he should have had that conversation with his doctor at Jefferson. I really didn't know why, but if he could, the BMT unit was the only place I would ever recommend anyone to have a stem cell transplant.

The echocardiogram was our second test of the day. The technician was also very kind and gentle, and when she looked at the letter from Dr. Anton, she commented that it did not refer to radiation to the chest area. Rather, it referred to the periaortic lymph node and the base of the lungs.

We returned to the PDH after the echo, and Billy was called to examination room number three, where we met with Dr.

Kushner's nurse practitioner, a very sweet person who immediately recognized Billy's fidgeting and realized he was uncomfortable. She was concerned about his dehydration. I told her I had been administering one liter of liquid to him daily at home for the past three days, and she told us to follow up with our doctors once we returned home. The audiogram was our last test of the day, and again, the technician was very kind. She brought Billy into a testing room that looked more like a booth. I was not permitted in the testing room and was told to return in about an hour. I took advantage of the time and went to the cafeteria for a bite to eat and a hot cup of coffee. When I returned to the testing area, Billy was not quite finished. When he did complete the test, he was tired and did not want anything to eat. I coaxed him to at least get something to drink and to at least take a look at the cafeteria. He did agree to a Gatorade and a soft pretzel.

We returned once again to the PDH area and waited a while to see Dr. Kushner, but he was busy, and it didn't appear we would get in to see him within a reasonable period of time. Billy wasn't feeling well, so we went home. I thought maybe I should have insisted on seeing Dr. Kushner, but if he felt Billy's dehydration was a serious issue, I thought he would have addressed it with me when we met with him earlier in the morning.

During those clouded months, I found myself questioning everything I did. I never knew if I was doing the right thing. I never wanted to be a bother, but then I never wanted things to get overlooked, as they had on several occasions. The second-guessing was part of my nature, and I suppose it was going to stay with me until someone had definite answers for us concerning this disease.

The ride home was uneventful, but the rest of the evening was not so good. Billy continued with the vomiting and coughing. Later, he started complaining of a sore throat from all of the coughing. In the morning, I tried to get Billy to eat some applesauce and drink Gatorade. He drank the Gatorade but refused the applesauce. I told Billy I would wait until noon to see if he would improve before I called the BMT unit. With his counts dropping, there was no way I was taking any chances. He began to recover and took it easy for a couple of days and rested, and his appetite slowly improved. Ryan drew labs, and his counts were stable, as was Billy's weight. Billy was laying low, not exerting himself, yet if he wanted to go out, he did. He just made sure he took a nap during the day and went to bed early at night.

●

March 12, 1999, was a cold, quiet Friday night. The boys were watching television, and I was catching up on some paperwork. Suddenly, the silence was broken with the ringing of the telephone. It was almost nine o'clock, and I figured it was for one of the boys, but none of them ran to answer it. I picked up the telephone and was surprised to hear Dr. Kushner on the other end. He had just received the test results of Billy's PET scan, and he didn't like them. I held my breath as he continued to speak. He said they were inconclusive, and he wanted to set up a CT scan for Billy. He asked how Billy was doing. I told him Billy was still not feeling well. He was still getting nauseous on a daily basis. Dr. Kushner said ideally he would like to try to cut back on his medications, but now probably was not the time. I agreed; there was no way we could stop his meds now.

I told Billy about my phone call with Dr. Kushner and that his office had set up an appointment for another CT scan, this time in New York. Billy wasn't thrilled about another trip to New York, but he was okay about treating with Dr. Kushner. He felt safe with him. Dr. Kushner had written the protocol, and he felt comfortable around him. Especially after talking with Bob McCarthy, Billy knew Dr. Kushner was the best doctor to treat DSRCT.

On Monday, March 22, 1999, Billy and I were back in New York for his CT scan, which was scheduled for 10:20 a.m. While waiting for the test, we met with Bob McCarthy at the day hospital. He had been communicating with us via the Internet. We had just discovered e-mail and found it to be an essential tool. Bob was finishing his radiation that Wednesday and was then scheduled to get a boost of his stem cells that Friday. He was hoping to go home the following Wednesday.

We had to cut our chat short with Bob, as Billy was called for his CT scan. Again, I waited in the waiting area, and shortly thereafter, Billy returned to where I was sitting, and we headed up to see Dr. Kushner, who was ready for us. He examined Billy and said he felt absolutely nothing in his neck. He felt Billy was making great progress, and he really wanted us to cut back on his medications. I said I would stop the Kytril that evening and observe Billy. If there were no adverse reactions, I was to discontinue the Kytril until further notice. Dr. Kushner felt that was a good place to start.

Dr. Kushner's eyes met Billy's, and he placed his hand on Billy's shoulder.

"Billy, you are really doing well. If I could grant you one wish, what would it be?"

"*Reverse this ileostomy!*"

Billy didn't even have to think about that. Dr. Kushner sat back for a minute and put his hands together, first interlocking his fingers with the index fingers pointing toward his lips. Then he put his right hand down, leaving his left on his chin, with his head nodding to the left. Suddenly he sat up and said, "I know just the person. I know what we are going to do."

Dr. Kushner made a telephone call to a colleague of his and set up a consult and evaluation with Dr. LaQuaglia. He said this doctor was very good and he would be better able to answer Billy's questions about reversing the ileostomy. He also advised Billy to continue his regular appointments with Dr. Folley. First and foremost, he wanted Billy to have a normal lifestyle routine. We received a call the very next day stating the scan of the neck was clean. We still had to wait for the chest, abdomen, and pelvis scans. They were not yet back.

Appointment with Dr. LaQuaglia, March 31, 1999

We made an appointment with Dr. LaQuaglia regarding the possibility of reconstructive surgery for Billy's ureters and to discuss what alternatives we had with respect to the ileostomy. Dr. LaQuaglia had an opportunity to speak with Dr. Berber on Tuesday, March 29, 1999. He said they spoke at great length. Dr. LaQuaglia was not satisfied enough with the CT scans and report from Dr. Berber to even consider reconstructive surgery. His first priority was to assess the status of the tumor remaining on the diaphragm, lungs, and liver. He needed to have this clarified by Dr. Kushner or Dr. Folley. There was a bit of confusion as to the status of the disease after the scans were done, so Dr. LaQuaglia suggested presenting Billy's case to the tumor board on Tuesday or Thursday of the following week. Either he or Dr. Kushner was to get back to us with their thoughts as to our next course of action after meeting with them. That sounded impressive to me—"the tumor board."

Dr. LaQuaglia explained to Billy that one could live quite a normal lifestyle with an ileostomy. It was not a life-threatening ailment. He also explained that one could live with the stent replacement every three months. It might be an inconvenience, but it was not life threatening. After reading through his notes on Billy's chart, he gave us a laundry list of things that he had done in the past with patients in similar situations, such as removing the diaphragm and replacing it with some sort of artificial device. This did have drawbacks, such as being short of breath, having decreased energy levels, etc. He said he had just performed a similar operation on a demo DSRCT patient within the last week or two prior to our visit. The doctor wasn't sure if this was something necessary for Billy at the time. However, he was just giving us possibilities of what could be done or what proved to be successful in the past for tumors on the diaphragm. He wanted to take a better look at the scans before rendering an opinion, as he was led to believe there was still tumor on the lungs. To the contrary, we were under the impression from Dr. Kushner after he took the last CT scan on Monday, March 22, 1999, that the lungs were clear. Dr. LaQuaglia also had to assess the tumor on the liver. We were aware there was a spot on the liver, but again, we were led to believe that was minimal as well. We were told we had no other choice but to wait until after all the tests results were in and reviewed by the tumor board to get a better picture of what was going on. Both Billy and I were anxious to hear from Dr. LaQuaglia and the findings of the tumor board.

When Billy and I arranged our trip to New York with Dr. LaQuaglia, Billy had also made plans with his Uncle Bob to spend the weekend in Connecticut. Since his uncle frequented New York City for his business, he arranged to meet us at the hospital, and he would take Billy home with him from there. We thought that would minimize the amount of travel time

Billy would have to spend in the car at one time, as the trip to Connecticut from New York City would have been equivalent to our trip back home to New Jersey. There was one small snag to our plans: Billy woke up that morning not feeling well. It was five thirty in the morning, and he had had a rough night, not being able to sleep very well, so I told him he didn't have to make up his mind right away. He didn't have to go to Connecticut if he did not feel up to it. Billy thought he might have just been tired and he would nap in the car during the two-hour trip to New York and play it by ear. He would pack for the trip and be prepared, just in case. He had oatmeal for breakfast and a piece of toast with a cup of tea. He brought his supplement drink with him for the ride. After we had met with Dr. LaQuaglia and were sent to his nurse practitioner for a physical assessment and blood work, Billy had to think about whether he was up to the trip. I gave Bob a heads-up earlier in the day, explaining that Billy wasn't feeling too well, and he said it was fine. He would be near the city for business, and he would probably come up to the hospital anyway to see Billy. He said it was okay if he didn't feel well enough for the trip. Billy wasn't sure what to do. He wasn't feeling well, and he didn't want to be at someone else's house and get sick. Then again, he didn't want to disappoint his uncle. It was only for two and a half days. The rest of the family was going up on Easter Sunday for dinner.

We went down to the nurse practitioner's office, and Billy told her he was not feeling well. He complained of an aching pain in his eye. It was hard to pinpoint, but it felt like it was actually in the eye. The practitioner asked if he had a history of migraines, which he did not, and she looked into his eye with a penlight. She said she couldn't see anything, and she asked him many questions such as did he see dots or spots or stars before his eyes or had any hazing or blurred vision. He said no to all the questions. She said she would mention it to Dr. LaQuaglia but didn't think it was anything to worry about, as she couldn't see anything. She then began to evaluate his weight loss and the issues causing it. Billy had lost another ten pounds, and she asked if his nausea and vomiting episodes were the cause. Billy reported some nausea and vomiting episodes but did not think it was the culprit at that time. He did, however, tell them that he had been off the TPN and hadn't been able to maintain his weight since. The nurse sent Billy down to the lab to draw blood and do a few tests, then back to Dr. LaQuaglia. We waited a few minutes before the doctor entered and said he was very concerned about Billy's nutrition. He wrote orders for Billy to get back on TPN immediately. I had to call Ryan, and he took care of the orders for that. Before leaving, Dr. LaQuaglia promised to call us as soon as he heard from the board and would make an appointment to go over all of the test results with us.

Easter in Connecticut

By the time we finished with all of our appointments, Bob was already in New York. Billy decided to go back to Connecticut with him, and we would be together for Easter and then bring him home. By the time Bob got to the hospital, though, Billy was really nauseous. He began vomiting in the street while we were putting his suitcases in Bob's truck. I was hesitant to let Billy go so far away. I believe he might have been hesitant too, as he asked how long a drive to Connecticut it would be. We assured Billy he did not have to go. As a matter of fact, we could have postponed the trip until he was feeling better. Billy said he wanted to go, as every time they planned a little visit like this one, he had always been disappointed because of being sick. So we agreed that he would go, but the very minute he called to come home or if he felt sick, I would run up to get him. I guess he needed to feel a little independent.

During our April office visit, Dr. Folley stressed the importance of Billy getting out more and enjoying life. He realized Billy had been through some very rough rounds of therapy and some extremely long months of weakened stamina and days with his head in a bucket. He wanted Billy to, in his words, "massage" his life. He knew what he proposed was not traditional oncology treatment, but he wanted the treatment to include a patient's lifestyle, or try to. So when Billy wanted to go, I had to let him make that decision. He had his medicines with him, and I was only a phone call away.

Dr. Folley increased the Valtrex two times a day to prevent shingles. He discontinued the Bactrim and the Diflucan, and Billy scheduled an appointment with urology for his stent replacements when he returned. Dr. Folley conferred with infectious disease for a more GI-friendly antibiotic that prevented UTIs. Billy was prescribed Propulsid before meals to help clear the intestines faster, and he was allowed to take Kytril in the morning again.

I called Billy the next morning. He didn't feel too good. He had a bagel for breakfast, but it didn't stay down. I made an appointment with Dr. Folley for Monday. I advised her of Billy's weight loss and eye pain, and she said she wouldn't wait for our appointment with Dr. Folley to start the TPN; she wanted to start it immediately. I advised her that Billy was in Connecticut, so she had JHIS deliver the TPN on Saturday. When I called Billy later in the evening, he asked if Janet had any idea of what the eye pain could be. I explained that it was too difficult to evaluate over the phone, but everyone thought of migraines. By ten o'clock that evening when I called Billy, he was feeling worse. I told Bob and Dawn he needed to have IV fluids to prevent dehydration. I had Dawn take his blood pressure and pulse. If he was dehydrated, he usually had a very rapid heart rate. If he wasn't better in the morning, I was bringing him home. He had to be seen. It was too difficult with him being far from home; I was a nervous wreck all night long. Dawn said she could get the IV fluids and administer them for Billy first thing in the morning, and they would call me before I left for work.

Bob and Dawn called me first thing in the morning. Dawn spoke with a friend of hers, a home-health-care nurse, who told Dawn to take Billy to the UConn ER to draw blood in case of infection. Dawn wanted my permission, and I made sure Billy felt comfortable before doing so. Dawn was also concerned about the eye pain and wanted to have that evaluated, as did I.

I waited all day to hear from them. I called the UConn emergency room about three o'clock in the afternoon, and they had just discharged Billy about five minutes prior. Finally, Dawn called me around five o'clock and said Billy had two abrasions on the cornea of his eye, which was causing the pain. His lab work was okay, and they gave him Zofran IV for the nausea, which Billy said helped. Later that evening, after Sean and I went to the Living Stations and made our Easter visit to Gran, we called Billy. We tried calling the house until twelve thirty a.m. At that time, Matthew called me for a ride home from work. When I returned from getting Matthew, we tried again, and still no answer. At that point we really thought they were on their way to bring Billy home. I waited up on the sofa almost all night.

When I woke up in the morning, there was no sign of Bob and Dawn. They weren't at my mother's, and there was still no answer on Bobby's phone. By this time, I was extremely uncomfortable. I was worried there was something wrong. Mom told me to relax; if something were wrong, they certainly would have called me. She thought maybe their phone lines were down or something. I tried calling the operator. She said their phone lines were fine. I was thinking of driving up to Connecticut but thought that if they were on their way down to New Jersey, we would miss each other. Mom told me to just stay here and wait. Reluctantly, I went to my part-time job. On my break I called home several times and called Mom's house, and still no one had heard from Bob or Dawn.

When I returned home from work, I tried Bob and Dawn's house again, and Bobby finally answered the phone; it turned out their ringer was accidentally turned off. I was relieved and angry at the same time. Billy was still not feeling well, and Bobby had to bring him back to the ER because his eye got worse, and a rash had developed. They thought it might have been a reaction from an eye patch he and Dawn had made, or maybe a reaction to the tape. After a physician examined him further, he found that Billy had an infection in his eye called herpes zoster, otherwise known as shingles. The antibiotic drops prescribed by the physician the day before had actually spread the infection faster, which was why Billy felt worse. Billy was then prescribed Valtrex and Percocet for pain. Once I heard this, I was ready to drive up to Connecticut and get Billy. I don't know why I didn't. He insisted he would be fine until the following day, which was Easter Sunday. He didn't want me to come. I don't know why. I can't second-guess myself now, but wish I did take the drive to Connecticut right then and there. Instead, I told him I would wait a few hours and call him again. I didn't want him to be uncomfortable away from home. This had been a long ordeal, and I wanted him comfortable, but I also wanted him home and with me.

Mom, Nicole, Matthew, Sean, and I attended the Easter vigil that evening, and we called Billy as soon as we returned home. He assured us he didn't feel too bad at that point. I had a very hard time falling asleep, though. I was worried all night about Billy. It would have been a lot easier if I just went up to get him. This was the first time he was sick and I wasn't there for him. I didn't know what to do. This time I let him make the decision, and if this was what he wanted, I had to honor his wishes. After all, he was almost twenty years old, but he had been through hell and back. I just wished I could have felt comfortable enough to sleep.

On Easter Sunday morning, the phone rang at eight o'clock. Bobby was on the other end of the phone, telling me Billy did not have a good night; he wasn't able to keep anything down. They wanted to make sure I had all the supplies necessary for the ride home. About ten minutes later, Bobby called me again. This time he was somberly telling me Billy was vomiting incessantly, and they wanted my approval to return him to the ER for a dose of IV Zofran for the ride home. Billy wasn't even able to talk to me on the phone. Of course, I told them to get him to the hospital, and I would get there as soon as I could.

I packed the IV Zofran in the car as well as his pillows and blankets. Nicole, Matt, and Sean took the ride up with me. When we arrived at Bobby's house, their car was gone. I knew Billy was still at the hospital. We entered the house. Mom and the rest of the family were sitting around the table for Easter dinner, and they told me the hospital wanted to admit Billy. There was no way I wanted Billy to be admitted in Connecticut. Part of me was angry for not going up there days ago at the first sign of him feeling worse than when he left with his Uncle Bob. Then I was mad that I didn't have him further evaluated at Jefferson or at Sloan-Kettering, but both facilities did look at his eye and didn't seem too concerned. Of course, it was just the beginning stages, and there were no visible signs of infection. Even the ER doctor at UConn first said it was scratches on his cornea.

I got myself to UConn. Mom went with me. We met with the ER physician, who presented Billy's status as a very serious matter. He said he spoke with Rocco back at Jeff, and he agreed it was in Billy's best interests to keep him at UConn. I was persistent in getting my son back to Philadelphia and asked the doctors what it was they would do for my son overnight there, that I could not do while transporting him back to Jefferson. They retorted he needed IV fluids and medication. I showed them I was prepared with the IV fluids, and since the antibiotic was to run every eight hours, I had more than enough time to get Billy back to Jefferson for his next dose. The doctor was insistent on keeping my Billy there. Politely, I thanked him for all he had done for Billy but told him I felt more comfortable with our hospital back home, where they had all of his records. I explained that we had an infectious disease team familiar with Billy's history and his various infections following his bone marrow transplant and chemotherapy/radiation treatments. The doctor's response was that he didn't want us to wait around at another ER for a bed, to which I was quick to reply that all he need do was make a phone call to the bone marrow transplant unit and confirm there was a bed waiting for Billy. I had just spoken with our team of doctors at Jefferson, and they assured me they would be ready and waiting for Billy. The doctor at UConn did indeed call the bone marrow unit doctors to confirm my story, but before the doctor would release Billy, he waited to consult with the medicine team, who agreed that it would be in Billy's best interest to return to Jefferson, where his records were, as he was not in any serious danger at that time.

After they gave Billy another dose of pain medication and supplied me with another bag of fluids and IV Zofran for the ride home, we were discharged. We brought Mom back to Bob and Dawn's house, gathered our things, and packed the car, which by the way I rented (a Lincoln Town Car) to provide a smooth ride home for Billy. I wasn't taking any chances of triggering nausea on the way home. We got on the road about six thirty and headed to Philadelphia. Billy and I arrived at Jefferson Hospital around eleven o'clock in the evening, and the staff was anxious to see us. They were getting concerned. They were under the assumption that we were leaving UConn and getting on the road around four o'clock. It didn't matter in the long run, though; we were all just so happy to have Billy back in familiar surroundings and to have our own doctors treating him.

Back at Jeff

oy was Billy's nurse, and she drew labs and took his vitals. He was started on IV fluids as the resident examined and evaluated Billy. Hyperalimentation (TPN) was ordered, and during the early hours of the morning they transfused a unit of blood, as Billy's hemoglobin was down to 8.9. He was started on Bactrim and acyclovir. The infectious disease doctor and an ophthalmologist from Wills Eye Hospital examined Billy, and there did not appear to be any vision problems. The eye itself looked okay, but the rash lasted several weeks, and the eye pain lasted a few months, as the doctors predicted.

After a few days on the antibiotics, the eye doctor said Billy's eye was doing fine. The infectious disease doctor visited Billy as well and said the infection seemed to be healing fine. She led us to believe he could be discharged within a day or two. After Billy was settled, I went to work for a few hours and left Bill, Matthew, and Sean at the hospital. Billy was happy to have the company, and they all seemed to enjoy their visit.

Nanci Rainey

A few days later, Billy was able to go home. The doctors wrote the discharge papers and made sure home infusion had appropriate supplies at our house, especially the TPN and acyclovir. I had to run it over a period of one hour, twice a day. I called the nursing station to get the exact time it was run in the hospital so I could keep the same schedule. They still wanted Billy's blood work done twice a week, and that was set up with Ryan. They told me Billy was still suffering from nausea and vomiting, and I was a little perturbed they sent him home without making sure he was able to keep his meds down by mouth, even though I knew how anxious Billy was to get home. Billy was not eating very well since he was discharged. He didn't complain of nausea or stomach pain, but I noticed his appetite was diminished. I was keeping a close eye on him, but it was difficult on the days I had to work.

The following Saturday I had to work a long day, as it was a special sale day. When I ran home at lunchtime to see Billy, he was not feeling well again. He wasn't able to eat more than a few spoonfuls of macaroni. He threw up during the early part of the evening. His cousin Jason stopped over after work for a short visit, and Billy was able to hold his own during his visit. Sean helped Billy run his medicine while I was at work.

Billy slept a good part of the next day. I had to work from one to six during the day so Mom stayed with Billy and brought him soft pretzels from Aunt Mary, but he was only able to eat a small part of one. When I returned home from work, I made him a little bit of soup, and then we watched a movie. By ten p.m., Billy was very tired and just wanted to go to bed. After I ran the Benadryl, he started throwing up and I was getting worried, but he told me he would be fine and he did sleep through the night.

Billy slept until almost one o'clock in the afternoon the next day. I ran his acyclovir before I went to work and disconnected his TPN. He was half-asleep while I flushed his lines, etc. It was a rainy day too, so that may have contributed to his not feeling well. He did get up once in the afternoon for a little bit of soup but then went back to sleep. When I went home for lunch, he wasn't hungry and wasn't feeling well again. I was glad our visit with the doctor was the next day. Our three-o'clock visit with Dr. Folley lasted until six o'clock; it was a very good visit. Dr. Folley was very receptive to Billy's needs, and he said he didn't care how often we saw Dr. Kushner, but he himself wanted to see Billy every two weeks. If it was the last thing he did, he wanted to get to the bottom of the nausea and vomiting matter. He and Lori put their heads together, and after a few phone calls, they came up with NegGram to replace the Bactrim. Billy's eye was very itchy, and Dr. Folley said it would itch as it healed, which was normal. We also discussed the issue of stent replacement versus reconstructive surgery. Dr. Folley had no objections or any reason why Billy couldn't have the procedure done, but it was Billy who requested to wait until after the summer. He wanted to ride his bike and get some work in. He didn't want to be laid up with a surgical procedure. We were all in agreement with this, and we arranged to have the stents replaced after Billy took the motor-cycle-driving test.

Friday evening, two days before we were having a dinner party for Billy's birthday, he, Sean, and I filled the back of Billy's pickup truck with the patio blocks from his former puppy's now vacant pen for Mom and Bob to use in their yard. (Shortly after Billy had been diagnosed, we had to surrender his dog, Rocky, as no one was home to care for him on a daily basis. It broke Billy's heart to see Rocky go, but it was best for the dog.) It had been raining all day but had stopped by dinnertime, and I, of course, with my OCD, thought it would be a great time to get the pen cleaned up and remove all of the cement blocks. Well, the weight of the patio blocks caused the truck to sink in the mud. Sean was left with the task of jacking up the truck. I tried to help him but to no avail. We started with the small jack and then had to retrieve Billy's big jack, when Billy jumped in. I was worried about him performing such strenuous activity, but I couldn't stop him. His adrenaline was working on overtime. He was just a bit angry with me. He wanted to get his truck out of the mud. We dug and dug and put blocks under the tires, etc., but when Billy tried to get the truck out, the blocks went flying, along with the mud. We all had mud spewed all over us. Billy was upset—to say the least. Sean and I felt completely helpless. We were all up to our knees in mud. We had been out there almost three hours, and Billy was frustrated. It broke my heart to see him so upset. I felt completely responsible. I was almost insistent on getting the blocks out of the yard. I couldn't let things go for another day. I should have listened to my son. He told me the ground was too soft. Oh, how sorry I felt that night. I don't know if he ever forgave me. It was a very frustrating night for him. He got so distressed, and I was praying he didn't get himself sick. We cleaned ourselves up, and I ran Billy's meds, then he went to bed. I told him how sorry I was, and he said it was okay. He said he would get Matt or someone from the yard to pull him out the next day; it was no big deal. He said, "Mom, I knew the ground was too soft. I should have known better than to load all those blocks in there. It's not your fault. Don't worry about it."

"Billy, you know I insisted on getting it done tonight. I'm sorry. Nobody's going to be outside tomorrow. Who's going to see the yard? You know me; I'm too impatient. I'm so sorry. I didn't want you to have to do anything but drive the truck. You can't get yourself sick; you can't. I love you, Billy. Good night."

"Good night, Mom."

"Let me know if you need anything, okay?"

"'Kay."

This was the first time I didn't care that I was covered in mud. I would have lain in the mud if I had to. I prayed for a miracle to get that truck out. One would hope that I learned a lesson that night, a lesson in patience. Well, I'm still trying.

crowded. The boys were enjoying the movie and suddenly there was a scene with a lot of racing, flashing lights, and loud noises. Sean heard Billy making sounds. After a while, Sean looked at Billy and realized he was not imitating the sounds of the movie. His eyes were glazed and he was not responding to him. Sean, only thirteen at the time, was frightened and not sure what to do. The patron in the seat behind him asked if he was okay and if he needed assistance. Sean shrugged his shoulders in puzzlement. He doesn't remember exactly what he did, but somehow, Sean made a phone call to me at home, and I immediately drove to the theater and took Billy to the emergency room. He was having a seizure. The doctors diagnosed it as a withdrawal seizure, brought on by the flashing lights and sounds from the movie. He was admitted to the hospital and observed over a period of two days. Needless to say, this is one movie Sean will never forget. I was very proud of Sean. He reacted calmly and quickly, and we were able to get Billy to safety.

After that hospital visit, when he was feeling better, Billy was serious about trading in his Honda dirt bike for a motorcycle. He had the cycle selected, and he couldn't wait to show me. I held my breath as I gazed at the bike he had chosen. A Suzuki 750 cc engine. It was a beautiful shade of blue, but it was a fast bike. I was frightened for my son to be out on the busy highways on this bike, but this was his dream. He wanted to live free and fear none. How could I tell my son a motorcycle was too dangerous after what he had been through? What could be more dangerous than chemotherapy and radiation?

After he purchased the bike, his friend Matt helped him hitch it to the back of his car, and they brought it home. The minute Billy passed his motorcycle test, he was on the road. I remember one Sunday afternoon, Mom and I were going to Grandmom's house, and Billy wanted to visit her as well. He followed us there on his bike, his first time over the Tacony-Palmyra Bridge on a motorcycle. I was in awe watching my son in the rearview mirror riding a motorcycle. He was happy as can be. Those are the days I want to remember.

On June 11, 1999, Billy was admitted for stent replacement. This time I sat in the small waiting area on the ninth floor. Dr. Shur assured me it would only be an hour or less. I sat then I paced the floor. An hour seems so much longer than sixty minutes when you are waiting for someone. Sixty minutes—that's thirty-six hundred seconds. I started counting as I paced the floor. Finally I was greeted by Dr. Shur's assistant, who reported the stent replacement went well. Billy was to follow up with the doctor in two weeks. After the stents were replaced, Billy's PICC line was removed. This gave Billy a little more freedom, one less appendage. He was discharged after two days without incident.

Toward the end of June, Billy started to slow down. He didn't have the energy or the spark he had displayed earlier in the month. His appetite was slowly decreasing, and he appeared drained. He was home for Matthew's birthday on the twenty-second. Matthew was so glad he was there to celebrate with him that year. It meant a lot to him to have his brother home. It meant a lot to all of us.

Obstruction Destruction

On July 5, 1999, Billy woke up with very bad stomach pains. At first I thought it was food related, as
we had gone to a diner late the night before and
shared a tuna sandwich, and fries with cheese. I found the fries to
be very greasy and had a stomachache myself after eating them.
Billy didn't eat much of the sandwich, but he did eat most of
the cheese fries. As the day progressed, so did his nausea and
vomiting. By six thirty at night, he felt so bad he asked me to
call the doctor. When I called the BMT unit, the nurse on call
paged Dr. Felix who instructed us to come right in, had the nurse
admit him, and the resident, Dr. Brian, evaluated Billy. He was
very concerned about Billy's discomfort; his exam was gentle, yet
thorough and complete. Billy's blood pressure was 104/44. The
doctor had him sit up a while and took his pressure again. This
time it was 131/60. Billy was started immediately on IV fluids,
and X-rays were ordered, which showed an obstruction, but it
did not involve the bowel. Dr. Brian knew Drs. Felix and Folley
would order further studies in the morning. Kytril and Ativan

were added to Billy's IV line, and the vomiting stopped by the time they started the second bag of fluids. Shortly after Billy received his medication, he was comfortable for the evening and finally able to sleep.

In the morning, Billy went to radiology for a CT scan. We were given results close to midnight, wherein the resident said it was a partial bowel obstruction. When I asked what was obstructing the bowel, she didn't know. When I asked where the obstruction was, she said large and small intestines. I reminded her that Billy no longer had his large intestines; they were removed in October 1997. The resident then said she wasn't sure because "they only had a fellow read the scan. The radiologist would read it in the morning."

I called the team the following day for the results of the scan and was told the results weren't in yet, so I called Dr. Berber's office, hoping she had possibly seen the scan results. But again, we hit a dead end. Another day passed, and still no scan results, so I called radiology myself. Of course, they wouldn't release the CT scan report to me, but they would send them to Dr. Kushner in New York. They just needed my consent. I faxed consent forms for Dr. Kushner, and I also faxed a consent form for a copy to be sent to my mother's office at work.

I called Dr. Kushner's office and told them Billy was in the hospital for a partial bowel obstruction and we were awaiting CT scan results. I asked them if it would be a problem for us to get a copy of the prior scans for comparison and was told I could have the films overnighted if I had a doctor from Jefferson request them. I then called Dr. Berber's office and told her we were awaiting her review of Billy's CT scan for a determination of the blockage and hoped that she would have read it. She responded someone from her office was reading it, and she had to read it herself before getting back to us.

Frustrated, I sent Dr. Folley's office a letter on July 8, asking if they needed the films from New York and why were they so concerned about the staging of the disease rather than the obstruction. The following day, I was told Dr. Folley was out sick, and Dr. Felix intercepted the letter and called me at work. She commented on my letter and said they needed to compare the films to determine how much was new disease and how much might be adhesions. She said it was almost a catch-22 situation. I was so confused about the whole situation. None of it made any sense to me. They wanted to see what was causing the blockage, yet they needed to see if adhesions were on prior films. Dr. Felix actually had Lori call New York for the films, and Dr. Felix informed me there were nodules in that area. She was not sure if they were causing the blockage, which was what they wanted to compare on the films, but they hadn't yet heard from Dr. Berber.

When I arrived at the hospital, Billy was down in X-ray because his pain was increasing, and they wanted to run another obstruction series. The morning labs revealed pancreatitis again, so no food or drink for that development. His platelets were high, so they had to give him heparin injections while he was in bed. Maribeth and Dan were there to lift Billy's spirits again, and Billy and Dan were exchanging motorcycle photos. I was so grateful for the nursing staff. I knew I could leave Billy in their hands and he would be safe. Before Maribeth left her shift, she reminded the doctors of the thalidomide. They had increased it to 250 milligrams.

When Dr. Folley finally went in to Billy's room the following day, he said they started vitamin supplements in the IV, called PPN. There were no lipids. He wanted to increase the thalidomide to three hundred milligrams. During his visit, Dr. Berber entered and said she would rather avoid surgery if at all possible. She did schedule an upper GI with a bowel follow-through to the GI tract through the bowels to see the kinks and obstructions. She said it could have been radiation damage to the bowel causing the problem or adhesions, and the option of surgical removal of structural obstruction would have set him back. Abdominal surgery, as Billy was quite aware, was rough recovering from. It causes more scar tissue and could sometimes progress the tumor balance they had maintained thus far. There was so much for all of us to consider at that time.

Dr. Berber met me later in the lounge to tell me she would rather avoid surgery. She said following her last examination of Billy's scans there was considerable disease present and that Billy had ascites in the abdomen again. I certainly thanked her for the heads-up about the surgery but wondered why, if she felt that way, it was even a consideration presented to my son.

During the next week, Dr. Folley continued to increase the thalidomide fifty milligrams every couple of days until he reached the therapeutic dose (four hundred milligrams). He wanted to keep Billy at that level for as long as he could tolerate it, which he seemed to be doing fairly well, despite his GI issues. But Billy was trying to make the most of it.

Billy had his PICC line and upper GI procedures scheduled for July 12, 1999. For the upper GI, Billy had to drink that chalky contrast liquid, which was supposed to travel down into the bowels. For some reason, radiology was waiting all afternoon, and the contrast hadn't gone through to the lower bowel area. They sent Billy back to his room and hoped if they waited another few hours, the contrast would travel. Around nine o'clock that night, they sent up a portable X-ray machine to Billy's room to see if the contrast had gone through. Once the portable X-ray machine and technician exited the room, transportation entered and took Billy to CVIR for his PICC line. When we arrived at CVIR, we were told we had an hour wait. I told them Billy was supposed to go to radiology for the second part of his upper GI with small bowel follow-through. Cardiovascular interventional radiology told me it would put him back another hour because of transportation. I asked if I could transport Billy myself, and they agreed, so I grabbed hold of one end of Billy's gurney and pushed him to X-ray, when they agreed to take him in the interim, while we waited for CVIR. The X-ray only took about fifteen minutes, so I grabbed the gurney again and pushed Billy through the halls back to CVIR when I was stopped by one of the transportation supervisors and asked what I was doing. I explained my situation, and he took over for me. Billy and I laughed about that one for days. I said I could add a new job description to my résumé as a transportation aide. I only hit a few corners.

The only good thing about sitting in CVIR until one in the morning was the fact that I had access to Billy's chart and was able to read it cover to cover. Since I had copies of every test, OR report, and lab report, there weren't too many surprises in his chart. There were a few scribbles difficult to decipher, but it was interesting to read the marginal notes.

While sitting in CVIR, someone from radiology said Billy needed to return at eight o'clock the following morning for one more X-ray. But when the team came in for rounds the next day, they had no knowledge of such test. They reported the tests were inconclusive though, and the part of the bowel they needed to look at was at the stoma. They were telling us at that point all the barium passed. His hemoglobin had been running low, so he was getting units of blood as needed. After they cycled the TPN and his blood sugars were normal, Billy was discharged.

Two days after that discharge, Billy woke up vomiting. I ran Kytril, Ativan, and then Benedryl. He wanted to sleep. He said the TPN kept him up all night because he had to constantly go to the bathroom. Ryan came early that day to change Billy's dressing, and he put extensions on his PICC line. While there, he also called to get a prescription for fentanyl. It took me from ten thirty in the morning until two thirty in the afternoon to get the doctor to write a script. Well, apparently he wrote the script. He was just too busy to bring it to the pharmacist. I immediately drove into to the city, went to the doctor's office to get the prescription, and then brought it to the pharmacy, where I had to wait an hour to have it filled, after which time I brought it home for my son.

That evening, I opted not to run the vitamins in his TPN, thinking that could have been the culprit causing the vomiting in the morning. Billy wasn't yet vomiting, but he was weak and nauseous and had been sleeping on the sofa. Even during the day, the nurse would come and draw labs, and then Billy would go back to sleep or watch TV for a little while and nap again. I decided to stop the thalidomide, not being sure if that would help the nausea or not. Little by little, I was adding the vitamins back to the TPN, and Billy would start his vomiting again, so I would stop with the vitamins. When I ran his morning meds, he would ask for Benedryl so he could nap. He said that was the only way he felt good. He would sleep a good part of the morning and part of the afternoon, and then he could tolerate the rest of the day.

On July 17, Billy began feeling better and he surprised us and said he wanted to take the trip to the zoo with us. Nicole's company was sponsoring an event at the zoo with a DJ and a caterer, and the new primate house was open. It was nice being out together as a family, but I could tell Billy wasn't feeling up to par. It was much too hot outside with only a little breeze. We tried to find a shady spot to sit, and we brought plenty of water, but there was so much walking from one exhibit to another. Finally, Billy admitted he had to leave. It was too much for him. He was getting nauseous, and he was afraid he was going to vomit. We took him straight home, and I started his IV meds, without the vitamins, and he went to sleep.

The nausea and vomiting continued, despite the fact I was no longer adding the vitamins to his TPN, and Billy was constantly asking for Benedryl in the early afternoons so he could sleep. He didn't want to take the fentanyl swab. He said it wasn't effective. Finally, one day he said he wanted to go to the hospital because they would give him Demerol and take care of his pain. He was at the end of his rope. We had a doctor appointment the next day anyway, so he said he would wait.

When we arrived at Dr. Folley's office in the morning, he sent Billy for an X-ray and then waited for the results, which was when we discovered all the barium did not pass. Billy told the doctor he was disgusted with feeling that way, and he wanted answers. There were too many questions unanswered.

"Dr. Folley, what is being done about the blockage? What is being done about the barium that didn't yet pass through my lower bowels? How long can I continue without food? How long am I supposed to feel this way without improvement?"

Before Dr. Folley could answer, I mentioned that Billy had developed a slight cough and occasional sneezing and asked if that could be related. I also raised my concern that a week prior, Billy had weighed 141 pounds versus the 131 pounds he weighed during that visit. The doctors were telling us there was a bowel obstruction, which was causing the vomiting, but they were waiting for confirmation of the scans to identify exactly where the blockage was. Billy hadn't been able to keep solid food down for almost a week, and he was getting discouraged.

Dr. Folley said he hadn't received the report from radiology. He sent them the two scans for comparison, and he would bring the report up to me as soon as he received it later that evening. I waited until ten o'clock that evening—no doctor, no report. The resident, however, came in a few times and explained why they didn't want to push the barium through with Maalox or Propulsid: because if it was a structural blockage and they pushed, it could have done more harm. He told us Dr. Berber was on vacation for two weeks, but her associate, Dr. Rose, was there to evaluate the situation.

I sat with Billy in his room for a few days, waiting for results of tests and doctors to come in and explain the results, neither of which happened in a timely manner. Billy encouraged me to go to work in the Philadelphia office. He said if someone came in with any news, he would call me, and I could run straight to the hospital and get the results with him. He said it was sometimes nice to have some downtime alone. Besides, he didn't want me to miss unnecessary time from work just sitting there and waiting. He knew I would run back to the hospital at lunchtime and leave work a little early to catch the doctors anyway.

By this time I had already quit my second job and my days at the office were getting far and few between, as Billy's hospitalizations were gradually increasing. I had to be with Billy. I couldn't deny the severity of the situation any longer. It was at that time I knew I needed a leave of absence. I had always thought Billy was just having a bad day, a bad week. He would get better tomorrow. "It's okay," I'd say. "He'll be better tomorrow. He's just having a bad day. It'll pass. He'll get his strength back. Give him time." And I truly did believe he would be better after this hurdle.

When Dr. Folley and the team finally evaluated Billy and radiology completed their report, we were told the scans appeared to be about the same—no better, no worse. There might have been a very slight increase in one or two of the nodules, one millimeter or two millimeters in size. Dr. Folley wanted Billy to start with the thalidomide again. Dr. Anton, the radiation oncologist, also evaluated Billy. She had a call in to the radiation oncologist at Sloan-Kettering to see how many of their patients with whole-abdomen radiation had been stricken with that type of obstruction. She believed it might have been chronic. Unfortunately, if Billy felt some relief and then tried to consume food, he could have suffered with that obstruction again. She agreed with Dr. Folley that it was too early to determine if Billy would be able to eat again. She reiterated what the surgeons said about not opening up the abdomen. She also said he had an abdomen of adhesions and scar tissue, and it would be very difficult to remove them. She said in some cases they were able to resection the bowel, but she wasn't sure what our options were here. She would know more after she heard from Sloan-Kettering.

Around ten o'clock in the morning, Dr. Felix made rounds with the team and relayed that Dr. Berber was only inserting the G-tube. Within a half hour, a surgeon from the GI team came to Billy's room and briefed us on the pending G-tube procedure. A doctor from the GI team entered the room shortly thereafter. His eyes were fixed on the chart, with an occasional glance in my direction. Then, hesitantly, the physician spoke softly, stating there was more disease present on the new films than the previous studies, and he felt the adhesions had progressively worsened within the past month. He recommended the G-tube for decompression of the stomach and explained that if the obstructions in the bowel didn't clear, Billy wouldn't have been able to eat. He also advised that solids would not pass through the tube, only liquids. The only way Billy would have been able to eat solids was if they cleared the bowel, and that seemed to be the biggest challenge. The GI surgeons were apprehensive to surgically clear the bowel. The risks were too great at that point. If they felt a lesion or a stricture could have been removed, they would have removed it, but they felt there were too many, and it would have eventually gotten worse.

After hearing the doctor ramble on with his grim view on what they anticipated, Billy got extremely upset and asked me to call Drs. Kushner and LaQuaglia in New York for their advice. Immediately I made the call but, unfortunately, was unable to speak with either of them personally. I left messages for both and awaited their calls. Billy was clearly depressed. He asked me to call New York again. Hours passed, and still no return call. We prayed together. It was a very emotional couple of hours. Billy had so many questions. He was so worried that he wouldn't be able to eat again. He wanted to know why they couldn't just operate and fix the problem. Why did Dr. Kushner say no surgery, only bowel rest? Was this before or after Friday's study? The questions went on and on. I had no answers for him. I couldn't explain why they were talking G-tube. All I understood was there were obstructions, and that didn't sound good to me. My heart was breaking. I prayed to the Holy Spirit for guidance and wisdom. Finally, I asked Billy to tell me what he would do if it were me needing these tubes and operations. What would he want me to do?

"I want to be able to eat. That's what I want."

"I know. I want that for you, too, Billy. Do you want to go through another surgery?"

Still no response. My prayers continued. "Come, Holy Spirit, guide us, protect us, give us the wisdom to make the right choices. My dear blessed Virgin Mary, our mother, through your intercession, I plead for your motherly love and the protection of all the angels and saints to watch over my son and guide the doctors and surgeons who may be treating my son. Amen. Protect us, Mother Theresa. We need a miracle. Sweet Jesus, please heal my baby. Thank you. Amen. Padre Pio, intercede for us, please."

Later that afternoon, Dr. Berber went to the room to speak with Billy and me. She told Billy she was going to perform the surgery and explained in detail what the surgery would entail. It was her intent to eliminate all or as much scar tissue as she could that wouldn't cause damage to him. She warned that if there was a lot of tumor, though, she couldn't guarantee anything could be done, but she would get a tissue sample for Dr. Kushner in New York for his study.

At three thirty in the afternoon of August 2, 1999, Billy and I were in the cold, stark holding area of the hospital when the anesthesiologist came and explained the type of anesthesia he was administering and a brief summary of the surgery being performed. He said Dr. Berber was going to try to remove any obstructing lesions and insert the gastric tube, with the surgical procedure taking an hour or two and then an hour or so in recovery. He told me this was as far as I could go, so I bent my head down, and said a prayer. I kissed Billy, told him to be strong and that he was my hero, and slipped him the green scapular, which he agreed to wear. On my way to the eighth-floor family waiting area, I saw the senior Dr. Rose and introduced myself. He was our surgeon's father, a retired surgeon himself, and said he was in to see Billy on Friday and he happened to be on his way to surgery "to see what Donna was doing." He told me they would try to make my son comfortable, though he didn't think there was a whole lot she (the surgeon) could do. I thanked him for his time and proceeded to the waiting area.

The nurse liaison had nothing to report initially, other than to suggest there was a question as to whether a procedure other than inserting a G-tube was scheduled. She was to clarify the procedure with the surgical unit and report back to us. The surgical team hadn't started until four. At six o'clock, Dr. Berber came to see me in the waiting room and said they had inserted the G-tube but were unable to remove any of the adhesions. His abdomen had quite a bit of tumor, and she couldn't safely manipulate any of it. She was, however, able to get a tissue sample to send to Dr. Kushner for the vaccine testing. She said Dr. Felix was in the OR and made sure the sample was frozen and sent.

I was permitted to stay with Billy in the recovery room, though he was heavily sedated. Afterward, he was brought back to his room, where we were met by Dr. Felix. She told me she had called Dr. Kushner, and they were all disappointed with today's findings. I too was disappointed and needed moral support. Tearfully, I called my mother and Bob, and they went right to the hospital to be with us. Later that evening, around nine o'clock, Kevin also went to the hospital to visit Billy. He was still heavily medicated, but he knew his friend was there; he always knew. I spent the night with Billy; he had a hard time sleeping. Despite all the pain medicine, he was still in a lot of pain. His basal rate of Dilaudid was up to seven. Then his respiratory rate dropped to seven. We stopped the Dilaudid PCA pump for a few hours to get his heart rate and respiratory rates back to normal levels.

BMT Party

For the first time in days, Billy was tolerating the pain and not vomiting. The nurses were waiting on him hand and foot. They just loved Billy, and the feeling was mutual. Billy had a full house of visitors stream in, starting with Kevin and his mom, then Nicole, Louisa, Matthew, Sean, and Josh. In a few days, Billy was drinking clears and progressing to a soft diet, so I ran to Wawa for an assortment of water, ice, yogurt, pudding, and anything soft he might want to try. Dr. Folley continued to check on Billy first thing in the morning, checking his labs and vitals, making sure his levels were all where they were supposed to be. In the meantime, Jack, one of the aides from the Bone Marrow Transplant (BMT) unit, was anxiously awaiting the BMT party at our house and handing out flyers with directions to all the employees. Everyone was excited for the appreciation bash Billy was hosting for the unit on August 8.

The day before Billy was to be discharged, he developed a fever of 102.9. The nurses were told to administer liquid Tylenol in the G-tube and clamp it for about an hour, hoping some of it would be absorbed. Knowing how anxious Billy was to go home, his doctor told us as long as Billy was fever-free for twenty-four hours, he would write the discharge orders. When Billy was finally discharged, he immediately began to make the final preparations for his party, which was scheduled just two days later. During the course of those next two days, Billy's pain levels were increased, and his fever spiked again. The visiting nurse had to administer liquid Tylenol in the G-tube again and let it sit for forty minutes. We were assured the G-tube wasn't blocked because it flushed fine. I continued to run the vancomycin and Dilaudid, but the nausea and dry heaves continued. Nicole spent most of the day running errands for me and Kevin cut the grass. Everyone was trying to get the party preparations finished. Billy was grateful for their help, but he was unable to sleep despite their efforts, so he dozed in his recliner with the massagers on. I slept on the floor next to his chair, and Kevin spent the night on the sofa near Billy. I think Billy slept off and on from maybe midnight to four o'clock in the morning with few interruptions. I was able to comfort Billy a little bit with a dose of Ativan.

When he awoke on the day of the BMT party, August 8, 1999, JHIS had sent two more nurses for follow-up care. They brought a new needle box and more Dilaudid. We were able to keep Billy comfortable until about noon, when Billy's staples began secreting stool. By the time I got that cleaned up, he started leaking again. His guests, which were most of the BMT unit staff that were not scheduled to work that day, started streaming in, with Dr. Folley being one of the first to arrive. He examined Billy, and we were in his room for over an hour trying to rig something up to collect the leakage while the guests were out in the yard, peeking in with curiosity. We told them to enjoy themselves and that Billy was fine. Dr. Folley then made a few phone calls and arranged for us to have Billy admitted at Jefferson. He did, however, allow Billy to entertain his guests for a few hours. Then we had to leave for the hospital.

We arrived at Jefferson around seven o'clock in the evening. Louisa and Kevin accompanied us to the hospital and spent the night until we received some results. Billy went down to X-ray for an obstruction series and a CT scan. Three different surgeons came to see Billy, and each had a different diagnosis. It seemed there was a ruptured part of the bowel causing a fistula to the suture site. Dr. Berber was to be consulted the following morning, most likely looking at surgery, but it didn't appear to be in the abdomen, no peritonitis.

The following morning, the surgeons consulted with radiology and Dr. Folley and said it wasn't a fistula. There was no leakage of the bowel. It had gone into the abdomen, causing peritonitis. They said they had to operate to drain the fluid. One doctor told Billy he didn't have to sign the consent to operate, but if nothing was done, the poison would kill him. Out of fear, Billy opted to sign the consent form, and we waited for an opening in the OR. Around eleven thirty in the morning, transportation arrived for Billy. We were in the holding area while the doctors and anesthesiologists conferred about the procedure. They told Billy and me he would wake up with the ventilator in his mouth and the NG tube up his nose. They didn't want him to wake up and be frightened when he saw the tubes.

Dr. Berber spoke with me before they brought Billy to the operating room. I stopped by the chapel before going to the family waiting area. Dr. Berber called about two thirty, saying they had found the problem. It was a portion of the bowel they had previously worked on, and it perforated. They inserted a JP drain, closed him up, and brought Billy to the intensive care unit. He was on the respirator and an NG tube and heavily sedated. He couldn't communicate at all. He knew we were there, though.

Billy's pain meds were reviewed by a pain-management team and adjusted accordingly. He was weaned off the respirator, and they removed it by noon the following day. The surgical team went to his room and checked on him several times the next day and cleaned and changed the packing on his wound. One of Billy's PICC lines was clogged, and we had to have the doctor try streptokinase. The nurses were not permitted to use that or heparin in the ICU. One of the nurses in the ICU gave me a hard time about staying with Billy and sent me home the second night, but everyone else was exceptionally nice and allowed me to stay. Billy had a lot of visitors from the BMT unit; Maribeth went in the mornings before her shift and evenings after her shift; Joy went Monday and Tuesday nights; and Jack came by three times. There was so much love and support from those guys in BMT. I could never repay them. My dream team!

After a few days and a lot of confusion, it was finally approved by Dr. Rose to move Billy back to the BMT, where he belonged. Again, he had a steady stream of visitors—Diane, Joseph, Terri, Nicole, Kevin, and Matthew, and Bill would bring Sean up when he could. There was a full house. The resident examined Billy and started his IV fluids and antibiotics. Billy was jaundiced, and his infections were serious. Peritonitis set in and he was septic. I was wondering why this kid couldn't catch a break.

The infectious disease team went in to see Billy early on August 12, and started him on the strongest antibiotics that covered a wide spectrum of bacteria to protect against all others. Afterward, I spoke with Dr. Berber in the hallway, and she said Billy was doing fine from a surgical standpoint. They were still running liver-function tests, as his bilirubin was 3.8. The other levels were within normal limits. His creatinine levels were elevated, and she was having nephrology look at them. Later in the afternoon, Billy was visited by Godmother Louisa, who brought party favors and streamers, as it had been her birthday and she wanted to celebrate and keep his mind off the hospital for just a short while.

My Rock

Billy was a little restless the next morning and out of sorts most of the day. The team felt he had a severe reaction to the pain medication. Therefore, they pulled off one hundred milligrams of the fentanyl patch. Billy continued to be delusional and have hallucinations, and he became combative. Maribeth and I sat up with him until two o'clock in the morning to calm him down. At three thirty we had to call Andy, the resident from the unit, to come to Billy's room. He increased the Dilaudid to three milligrams and gave him one milligram of Ativan, and that seemed to work for a couple of hours. The combination of the increased fentanyl and Dilaudid made Billy really reactive, and when we removed one hundred milligrams of fentanyl, he went into withdrawal. It took a while to clear his system as long as his liver functions were sluggish.

Billy's right leg and ankle were swollen, and the doctors ordered an ultrasound to rule out blood clots. The ultrasounds of the liver and kidneys were also negative. There were no blocked bile ducts in the liver. Things just seemed sluggish from the trauma. Billy became more paranoid, combative, and then he got melancholy as we tried to calm him. Louisa, Regina, Nicole, and Bill witnessed a lot of this, and it upset them terribly. Mom went to the hospital early the next morning and witnessed Billy still fighting the withdrawal symptoms. I know it broke her heart to see him like that. Denise gave him Ativan, and he became quiet and slept off and on most of the day. While awake, Billy prayed with us. Bob and Dawn joined us in the afternoon as well as Nicole. Silently I prayed, "Dear Lord, I love my baby. I pray he gets strong soon so we can take him home."

Billy looked much better with each passing day. He was even drinking soda. His pain was finally under control. We put a few movies on, changed his dressings, and settled in for the night. Around one o'clock in the morning, Billy started moaning in his sleep, and when I looked over, his sutures had started leaking again. I called for Maribeth, who in turn called for the resident. Franz came in as quickly as he could to examine Billy, then called the surgical team. Dennis came in to help Maribeth and me clean the leakage. Dr. Rose was on call and said he was strongly opposed to surgical intervention.

On August 16, almost two o'clock in the morning, we made a custom-fit wafer from the surgical supplies and placed an ostomy bag over the opening of the leak. It was going on four o'clock in the morning, and we were still waiting for Dr. Berber or Dr. Folley to examine Billy. When Dr. Folley came in, he assured Billy of his promise to keep him comfortable. Much later that morning, after Dr. Berber and Dr. Folley conferred, Dr. Folley asked the team to join him as well as me in the conference room. He explained the situation and said we could do a CT scan or X-rays to find the leakage, but because of the risk to Billy, they couldn't operate at all. If the bowel had formed a fistula to the opening, it would have been ideal, but if it leaked and fluid secreted to the abdomen, peritonitis would have set in. They would have added another antibiotic, Unasyn, which should have covered about all the infections going on. If possible, they would like to have seen Billy go home, but if the fevers, infections, and new things continued to develop, he would have to stay at the hospital. Dr. Folley didn't think I should have had the added burden of diagnosing future problems that might have arisen. Dr. Folley advised me that Billy's time was very limited at that point, maybe weeks, not months. He said that if the peritonitis started leaking into the abdomen rather than out of the body, we might only have had days. With tears in my eyes, I shook my head. "No. No, you can't mean that. He will get better, you'll see. He will. He was starting to feel so much better. He was fine yesterday."

Dr. Folley cried and held me and said he was sorry. I was stunned and couldn't move. I wouldn't allow myself to believe him. There was no way my son only had days, maybe weeks. There had to be a mistake. How could I handle this? How could this be true?

"Oh, my God. Oh, my sweet, dear Jesus, please help me. Please come to my aide. Please help my son. Save my son."

I called Bill and told him he should be at the hospital. I called my mother, Kevin, Bob Lee, Dominic, and Matt Hinkel as well. Billy wasn't comfortable at all. His right leg was still swollen, and he was having difficulty breathing. They took another chest X-ray, but there was no change, still effusion. Mom came up with Matthew and Sean, and they spent the day with me. A little later in the afternoon, I had the boys run a few errands, just to get them outside for a little while and keep them occupied. After dinner, Kevin and his mom and dad stopped in for a visit, and my brother Joseph and his fiancé, Terri, also spent a good part of the evening with Billy. Once most of the visitors left, Kevin decided to spend the night with the boys and me. We managed with the window seat and the chairs. The nurses supplied pillows and blankets, and the boys were comfortable.

Billy was up most of the following day, as he had a steady stream of visitors. Bob Lee, Jim Hill, Matt Henkel, Dominic,

Diane, and, of course, Mom returned in the afternoon, and Kevin and the boys were still there with me. His breathing was less labored, and his spirits seemed to have been lifted, though it was difficult to tell with all of the medication. It was evident Billy was fighting his sleep. He wanted to be a part of his company's conversations, yet he was exhausted. By seven o'clock, when the nurse ran his Ativan and Benedryl, he was off to sleep. They raised his Dilaudid to a basal rate of four milligrams, and he slept until eleven or so, and then he had a hard time sleeping during the night. Between twelve thirty and one o'clock in the morning, Billy started with the shakes, and I called Dennis, his nurse on duty, who felt it was from the Abelcet antibiotic (a new one for me), which was for a fungal infection. Neither of us got much sleep that night.

I knew Billy was still experiencing depressive moments. He would try to hide them when he had company, but I could see it in his eyes. He was not feeling himself, and he wanted to go home. When we were alone, Billy and I started a conversation concerning his treatments and what was next. He asked what our next move was and if Dr. Kushner had any more research, or if he had gotten back to Dr. Berber or Dr. Folley. I got up as close to Billy as I could, and I said to him, "Billy, you are my rock. We're not going to give up."

He responded, "Mom, you are my shoulders." We just looked deep into each other's eyes, holding back the tears, and then I held him for as long as I could. Billy's eyes were closed, and I got up slowly, tiptoeing out of the room, knowing each of us needed a few minutes alone.

Out in the hall, I was approached by Dr. Folley, Maribeth, and Jan, the social worker, who wanted to discuss Billy's pending discharge. I was taken aback, as there had been no previous talk of discharge prior to that time. Dr. Folley felt that as long as JHIS could arrange a hospital bed, oxygen, and suction, there was no reason we couldn't get Billy home, as long as I was up to the responsibility. There was no question I was up to having my son come home, no matter what the challenge, and I told them to do whatever they needed to get it in motion. In the meantime, I made a few phone calls on my end to get things moving at home. I wanted Billy's room refreshed and renewed for his homecoming.

Meanwhile, lying in the hospital, anxiously waiting for the day of his discharge, Billy started staying up more during the day and seemed to be back to his good old self. Of course, he was looking forward to visiting with his pop. My dad was coming in from Nevada for my brother's wedding, and Terri, Uncle Joe's fiancée, had recently visited Billy at the hospital and surprised him with the news that she was getting Pop from the airport and bringing him to our house. She also told him he would be staying with us for a few days. Pop had been in Nevada for a few years, and Billy was excited to see him.

August 22, 1999, Dr. Felix examined Billy prior to discharge and went over his home-care needs. She explained to me the flushing of the PICC lines, the oxygen levels, the suction on the drains, and watching for blood clots blocking the catheter. Since Billy still got nauseous at night, he would continue to need Ativan and Benadryl in addition to the Dilaudid. While we were still in the hospital, a home-care nursing agency called me and scheduled fifteen hours a week home care. That day I figured we needed a few weeks to take care of Billy. It might take him a little longer to get better this time. He was really weak. It wasn't going to be tomorrow, maybe a few weeks. That was all—just a few weeks, and we would get him better. He was a fighter. Still believing we were going to make it, I wouldn't face the obvious. I continued to tell myself, "Once he gets home, he will be more comfortable. He will be in his own surroundings, and he will regain strength. We came this far. We're going all the way. After all, we have at least five years, right? Don't we have five years? Oh, please Lord, let us have the full five years. By then they will have more research. Please, let us get through this. Give Billy strength. Give me strength, please."

I continued to run to St. John's in the mornings as long as we were at the hospital. It was my shot in the arm, so to speak, to get through the day. I was pretty sure God was listening, though I wanted to make sure he heard me. Besides, Padre Pio was there, looking back at me with his eyes. Billy was intrigued with Padre Pio, so I knew he was listening to my prayers. He was taking care of my son. I just knew it.

Closing Time

On the evening of September 6, 1999, after I had taken my bath, Billy was not feeling well, and I asked him if he wanted me to lie with him for a while. I climbed onto the bed and nuzzled next to him. I prayed the Our Father with him, and I saw how weak he was, so I continued to pray silently. I asked him if there was anything I could get for him. With a shake of his head, I just softly rubbed his back. He had lost so much weight I was afraid I was going to hurt him. Suddenly his breathing became labored, and the rhythm of the pumps was getting irregular. I paused a moment to monitor his breathing patterns, which were now getting irregular—first rapid, then slower.

Sean and Kevin were there, and I knew it was time to call Matthew and Nicole home. I had to call Matthew home from work. Only God knows what he was thinking as he walked down the street to our house, hoping he would get there in time. My daughter was coming from Blackwood. She was hours from delivering her first baby, and I had to call my mother. Gathered together around Billy's bed, we held hands and prayed. With tears streaming down my face, I whispered in Billy's ear. I told him I loved him so much. I told him how strong he was, how sorry I was, how I wished I could have done more for him. He whispered "I love you, Mom. Thank you." His eyes, half-closed, scanned the room, gazing at the circle of love surrounding him. He knew we were there. He knew how much we loved him and how much we wanted to fight for him.

At first I told him to hang on. I told him he would be better tomorrow, if he could just hang on. We'd been through this before. He had a few bad days, and we managed to survive those perils. We could make it through one more. But this time, he really didn't look good. Something about his breathing and his coloring put me in panic mode, and I wasn't sure what to do. Against the loving counsel of the doctor and my mom, there was no way I would let go. What mother would do that? I couldn't believe they even suggested I do that, but I didn't know what to do. I prayed as I lay there holding Billy. I could hear the beating of his heart, first in harmony with mine, then becoming more irregular, first a bit faster, then slowing down. After listening quietly for some time, I couldn't bring myself to ask, but I knew I had to ask. Softly the words came out. "Billy, do you see the light? Is there a light? Are there angels waiting for you?" Once I asked him, he looked at me, nodded his head, and barely whispered a yes.

I will never forget his last loving gaze into my eyes. He didn't want to leave me, but he had to. Hesitantly, I told him it was okay to go. He needed to hear it from me before he could let go of this world and enter the golden gates. The hardest thing I ever had to do was let my son go, to tell him I loved him, and release him to the loving arms of the angels sent to greet him. The second hardest was to relive these moments in this narrative, but it is all in Billy's memory, and may his memory live on forever.

Epilogue

Mesmerized by the glistening water in the distance, I was startled by the long, blaring bellow of the ship's horn. In an attempt to keep from stumbling, I shifted my feet on the wet, wooden planks and held tightly onto the rusty railing of the passenger deck. My eyes squinted as I shielded them from the prisms of sun mirroring across the water. Fighting back tears, I reflected on the life that was and mourned that which could have been.

It was a crisp September morning, and after attending a special mass dedicated to Billy, I embarked upon the Cape May Lewes Ferry as I had for the past ten years. I discovered serenity aboard the vessel on the first anniversary of Billy's parting and have since made it my own annual respite. A calmness grew within me while aboard the *M.V. Cape May*, traversing seventeen miles across the Delaware Bay. I stared straight ahead while the corner of my eye caught the wake of foam that trailed behind the vessel. There was an occasional school of dolphins cascading across the water and a glimpse of both the Cape May and Delaware breakwater lighthouses. The engines' constant hum drowned out the chatter from fellow passengers, leaving my thoughts totally focused on our family dynamics and how it had been so drastically changed.

The transformation began when I presented Billy, only eighteen years old, to our family doctor for complaints of abdominal pain. He calmly indicated there was nothing to be concerned with, claiming it was simply a pulled muscle that would be remedied with aspirin and rest. After two weeks of continued nagging pain, we consulted with a second doctor, who diagnosed his symptoms as a possible hernia and referred us to a surgeon, who, upon examination, did not find a hernia; rather, he felt there was an abnormality within the lymph nodes. I immediately sought a third opinion, and subsequently my son was sent for diagnostic studies and a complete blood panel series. Every test seemed inconclusive and warranted further studies, until ultimately he was sent for a CT scan and an MRI. Within hours after undergoing the radiographic tests, our doctor telephoned us with the dreadful news that there was a large mass within my son's abdomen. He immediately arranged for Billy's admission into the hospital for a biopsy, which required an incision through the abdominal wall; the physician's tone was serious, and he shared his concerns regarding both the size and location of the growth. Consequently, the biopsy report revealed cells characteristic of a very rare form of cancer, and it was imperative we proceed quickly with treatment.

Fortunately, our doctor could recommend a few specialists in the metropolitan area. Within a week's time, I was holding my son's hand in the pre-op room at Jefferson Hospital, where he was being prepped for yet another surgery, this time an invasive tumor debulking. The surgeons were astounded with the size of the tumor and the extent of its damage to Billy's internal organs. The tumor, extremely large, weighed in at fifteen pounds, and the doctors were forced to remove a large part of his intestines and colon, leaving my son with a permanent ileostomy. The surgeons felt they operated just in time; had we waited any longer, it might have been fatal.

Results of the pathology report confirmed the cell properties of the tumor were of an extremely unusual species, specifically, desmoplastic small round cell tumor (DSRCT). Information on this particular strain of cancer cells was limited, but fortunately, we contacted a doctor in New York City who had discovered a protocol for treatment of DSRCT. Unfortunately, though, we also learned through research literature, that the survival rate for DSRCT was reportedly only five years. Immediately we petitioned family and friends for their prayers. We needed a miracle.

Billy underwent six rounds of intense chemotherapy, all of which required three to four days' hospitalization. Following each round of chemo, Billy needed blood and platelet infusions, as the chemotherapy destroyed his good cells along with the bad. Usually within ten days after each round of chemotherapy, Billy's blood counts would drop to zero levels, compromising his immune system. At that point, my son required daily injections of cell-producing serum into his abdomen, which I immediately learned to administer. Along with the physical and permanent changes to his body following the surgery, as well as the loss of his hair and depleted stamina from the chemotherapy, Billy was plagued with intolerable pain and constant nausea and headaches. He experienced bouts of vomiting so severe it was necessary for him to have protein supplements dispensed intravenously with the use of a portable pump. At the young age of eighteen, Billy was literally fighting to survive on a daily basis. Every phase of his treatment was accompanied by side effects, and it seemed we always encountered another hurdle, often under the guise of an infection.

The most difficult and final stage of the protocol was the autologous bone marrow transplant and the six-week hospitalization in a totally sterile environment within the bone marrow unit. Billy's stem cells were collected after undergoing six weeks of radiation therapy, in the hopes of collecting "clean" cells. The stem cells were then frozen until the appropriate time for the transplant, which occurred after he completed three subsequent chemotherapy treatments. Each stage of the protocol was dependent upon his white and red cell counts being within a particular range, all the while under the close supervision of the New York specialist. In spite of the fact he was fighting against the odds, Billy continued to have faith. Regardless of the obvious physical changes from the ileostomy, and the side effects of the toxic medications, he was determined to win the battle and vowed to live strong. Even when his body succumbed to weakness and sheer exhaustion, Billy never once gave up hope. His love for life was great, and he was blessed with tremendous courage and inner strength.

During a very brief remission, he even managed to land a six-foot sailfish while on a fishing excursion in the Florida Keys. He also traded his dirt bike for a seven hundred fifty cc engine motorcycle, but shortly thereafter, his strength diminished, and he had to retire his new toy with only one hundred fifty miles on the odometer. Tragically, despite our prayers and the efforts of our expert physicians, Billy surrendered to the beckoning light and was released peacefully from my loving arms on September 7, 1999.

Each painful memory of my son's suffering caused me to shudder and wince, and I wondered why it was he who had to endure so much pain. After losing Billy, I didn't feel worthy of happiness, nor did I believe I would ever find joy again. I felt a sense of disloyalty to my son if I dared to smile or if I participated in any type of celebration.

With bittersweet irony, my emotions were pushed to the limit when, less than twenty-four hours after surrendering my Billy, my daughter gave birth to her first child. For a few brief hours, our grief was paused to experience the miracle of life. My daughter, who only hours prior had said good-bye to her brother—

more like a best friend—held her newborn baby girl in her arms. Whether the tears streaming down her face were of joy or sorrow, no one would ever know. My boys, just embarking on their teen years, were torn between visiting their sister and new niece at the hospital or assisting me with arrangements for their brother's funeral. None of us knew what we were supposed to do or where we were supposed to be, but through the grace of God, we managed to squirm through the week, and it wasn't until after the funeral that I collapsed.

Sorrow resonated through the empty rooms of the house now vacated by family and friends. We were suddenly alone with lingering memories and photographs, the silence interrupted only upon an occasional delivery person. Except for our immediate family, everyone else managed to continue with their own lives; they were able to move on and pick up where they left off. As hard as it was, my own children had to get back into the routine of life; the boys had to return to school, and my daughter had to begin a life of motherhood. I grew comfortable clinging to anger and sadness and fear of surviving without my son. His pleading words of "I want to live" echoed repeatedly in my mind.

I didn't know how to cope with the failure to save my son, and daily life became an excuse to simply exist one breath at a time. Slowly, I pulled back from the world, hoping I would wake up from this bad dream. But the nightmare continued. I couldn't escape my sorrow, and I wanted to be left alone. In my seclusion, I managed to isolate myself from everyone, including my children. Being so overcome with depression and being emotionally unstable, I wasn't available to them. The more time passed, the deeper into the depression I sank; even a trip to the grocery store would warrant hiding behind my sunglasses and keeping my head down to avoid eye contact with anyone in my path. Family and friends were concerned, but the more they reached out to me, the stronger I resisted. Veiled in my own corner of the world, I resented anyone who even thought they could remotely relate to my loss. My children, frustrated with my behavior, eventually began to withdraw to their rooms, altering our family dynamics further into unhealthy chaos. We were the epitome of dysfunction. The only thing I was capable of doing during those first few years was repeating and reviewing my son's short lifetime of memories and asking why.

Seeking mediums and learning meditation tactics temporarily appeased my longing to be with my son if I could feel his presence and believe the signs were indeed from him. My obsession with life on the other side further enabled me to continue living in the past and lose all interest in the present. Rather than confront my fears and sadness, I chose to cling to them; I was determined to do everything in my power to find a way to keep my son by my side.

It wasn't until my middle son tangled with the law five years later, disaster staring us in the face again, that I realized some things did indeed have to change, starting with me. My children were no longer babies I could protect from the safety of our home. They had grown up, and the world was now their playpen, surrounded by woven barriers of peer pressure and temptation. And where was I? How could I have let this happen? It was time for me to emerge from my cocoon and face reality, time for me to interrupt the silence and resume social ties. This was my wake up call. If I didn't come out of hiding, I might have lost yet another son.

Through the help of counselors and support groups, and the grace of God, my healing began. It was a slow process, a long and arduous journey upon which I was not alone. My son's very love for life was my incentive to continue on, to share the todays and any tomorrows that were to be; I never could have climbed out of the tunnel I had dug myself in without the help of Billy's friends. They would come to visit me, and I would hold back the tears, but eventually the floodgates would open. I knew it made them uncomfortable, and little by little, their visits became fewer and far between. That wasn't what I wanted. I wanted his friends to continue coming to the house.

I wanted things to remain as they were. But then I faced reality. Things cannot remain the same. Time cannot stand still. We cannot go back, we must move forward, like it or not. His friends wanted to visit me, but they did not want to see me cry, they wanted to move on. Indeed, they had moved on; they were young; they had their whole lives ahead of them. It wasn't fair to Billy or his friends to focus on the sad times. I was keeping the good old days buried deep inside of me. I was holding on tightly to Billy's memories and not allowing myself to share them with others. He was much too important to so many people to have me shut them out of my life now. I had to let his legacy live on, and the only way to do that was to let his memories escape from the deep crevices of my broken heart, to change my thinking from it being an invasion of the privacy of my heart to a desirable act of unselfish generosity for others to share.

I know now I can never lose my Billy again. My heart will try to mend around the breaks and bruises, and know it will always have tender spots, but in time, it will mend. I will still have my teary-eyed days, but I will also share some of my fondest memories of Billy with anyone who will listen. My heart is open, and I will love my children, always and forever. We've been through so much, but we've been through it together. My children are the greatest support system one could ever ask for. The memories we have to share—past, present, and future—will be cherished moment by moment. Friends will continue to visit, and we will share fond memories together. Some of Billy's friends have even honored him by sharing his namesake with their children. I shared tears of joy with them and continue to be honored by their thoughtfulness. I know Billy is smiling down on them.

Ironically, my heart and my eyes have been opened to learn that the son I was trying to save was the son who ultimately saved me. He intervened and gave me the peace in my heart and the strength to endure these last few years. He was my rock during his twenty-three month challenge. It was I who held onto him, but he was the one in the driver's seat; he had all the strength. He was the fighter; I was just his voice. He was and always will be the very angel walking by my side, guiding me and showing me the way to live our remaining days. As quoted by Padre Pio, "Near us is a celestial spirit, who, from the cradle to the tomb, does not leave us for an instant, guides us, protects us as a friend, a brother; will always be a consolation to us especially in our saddest moments."

When I find it difficult to handle a particular situation or day without Billy, I close my eyes and hum the lyrics of a song he was fond of, and somehow, someway I find solace to know my Billy is where he is supposed to be.

And still watching over me…my son, my angel, my best friend.

> Closing time, every new beginning comes from some other beginning's end…
> Take me home…
>
> Lyrics from Semisonic

Endnotes

1   Kushner BH, LaQuaglia MP, Wollner N, et al.: Desmoplastic small cell tumor: prolonged progression-free survival with aggressive multimodality therapy. Journal of Clinical Oncology 14(5):2526-1531, 1996.

2   Gerald WL, MD,PhD; Miller HK, MD; Battifora H,MD; Miettinen M,MD; Silva EG,MD; Rosai J,MD; Intra-abdominal Desmoplastic Small Round-Cell Tumor. Am J Surg Pathol 15(6): 499-513. 1991.

3   Kushner BH, LaQuaglia MP, Wollner N, et al. Desmoplastic small round-cell tumor: prolonged progression-free survival with aggressive multimodality therapy, Journal of Clinical Oncology 14(5):1526-1531, 1996.

4   www.dsrct.com/haleyhendricks.html

5   Ibid Kushner BH et al

6   "Genetics of Small Round Cell Tumors of Children" by Mohammed Akhtar, MD, FCAP, FRCPA and M. Anwar Iqbal, PhD, FACMG

7   ddenault@intap.net